T0162871

BORN MAD

Robyn Wheeler

Balboa Press books may be ordered through booksellers or by contacting:

Balboa Press
A Division of Hay House
1663 Liberty Drive
Bloomington, IN 47403
www.balboapress.com
1-(877) 407-4847

Because of the dynamic nature of the Internet, any web addresses or links contained in this book may have changed since publication and may no longer be valid. The views expressed in this work are solely those of the author and do not necessarily reflect the views of the publisher, and the publisher hereby disclaims any responsibility for them.

The author of this book does not dispense medical advice or prescribe the use of any technique as a form of treatment for physical, emotional, or medical problems without the advice of a physician, either directly or indirectly. The intent of the author is only to offer information of a general nature to help you in your quest for emotional and spiritual well-being. In the event you use any of the information in this book for yourself, which is your constitutional right, the author and the publisher assume no responsibility for your actions.

ISBN: 978-1-4525-3640-8 (sc)
ISBN: 978-1-4525-3642-2 (hc)
ISBN: 978-1-4525-3641-5 (e)

Library of Congress Control Number: 2011911787

Printed in the United States of America

Balboa Press rev. date: 07/14/2011

To my family, friends, colleagues, and therapists for their love, support, and advice, as well as for their understanding, during the strife and difficult times.

For those of you who suffer from anger and depression, may you find peace, hope, and happiness.

You will not be punished *for* your anger,
you will be punished *by* your anger.

-Buddha

Contents

Foreword
Courage and Determination

As Robyn's husband, best friend, and constant companion, I knew something was wrong, but I wasn't aware of the scope and magnitude of the problem. I tend to see the positive side of people; I forgive easily and, above all, I love my wife. When things seemed to go wrong, I just knew everything would work out in the end.

I only wish I had known then how bad things actually were. There were days when we exchanged only a few words. That's how I knew she was having a bad day—and she had a lot of bad days.

Because of my wife's courage and determination to get to the bottom of things, she is a different person today, and I am so proud of her. Read about her journey back from despair, and maybe her story can help save a marriage or a life.

Ron Wheeler

Acknowledgments

Thank you to my husband, Ron, for your never-ending love, encouragement, and support with this project.

To my counselors and therapists, thank you for listening to my problems and angst, taking me seriously, and giving me great advice. Please keep doing what you do.

To my editors, Andrea Glass and Lynette Smith, thank you for answering my constant questions and providing your superior services.

To all my family members, I love you and wish you an eternity of love, peace, and happiness.

To Hay House and Balboa Press, thank you for all the wonderful services you provide; you are making a positive difference in lives all over the globe.

To Dr. Wayne Dyer for being such a huge influence on my new life. Your *Everday Wisdom* and *101 Ways to Transform Your Life* have indeed transformed my life forever. You have my love, respect, and gratitude for eternity.

To my readers, I wish you an anxiety-free, joy-filled life of love, peace, and happiness.

….and to God, for His blessing, protection, guidance and forgiveness to all of us here on earth.

Part One

Just Call Me Firebucket!

Introduction

Born Mad is about anger. Not the fleeting anger that for a second or a minute makes you irritated. Not the anger you feel when someone cuts you off in traffic, when you burn a meal, when your teenager comes home past curfew, or when your spouse spends too much money. It's about chronic anger. The type of anger that consumes your life and forces you to make poor decisions or use bad judgment. The anger you can't get rid of, that takes over your every thought, night and day, for years of your life. It is about the chronic anger that makes you unable to forgive or to live in the moment and makes you relive past wrongdoings over and over again. The kind of anger that you turn inward, overwhelming yourself with feelings of worthlessness and of not being good enough, an anger that steals your happiness and self-esteem, your compassion for others, and lessens your quality of life.

If you don't suffer from chronic anger, be grateful you will never know what it feels like.

Born Mad is also about chronic depression and anxiety. Not major depression, when a person can't get out of bed or function on a day-to-day basis, but a mild, low-grade depression that often goes undetected for years by friends, family, physicians, and even the person suffering from it.

Dysthymia (pronounced *dis-thahy-mee-uh*) is the kind of chronic, low-grade, long-lasting depression that can cause either poor decision-making skills or a propensity for choosing the worst option in a situation; it can cause frustration, sleeplessness, worry, or extreme anticipation. It makes every day difficult, so you feel like you're swimming upstream against the current while everyone else is swimming downstream with the current.

You never reach the top, no matter how hard you try. It seems you're never as happy as the other guy, and all you really want to do is say, "I quit!"

If you suffer from dysthymia, you are probably happy most of the time. When nothing goes wrong, life is great, and you go about your daily life without a hitch. You hold down a job, run errands, attend to your children, and enjoy all the activities depression-free people engage in.

But when events happen that seem bad, harmful, or unpleasant, the depression sets in, making circumstances feel more severe for people with dysthymia than others. When multiple mishaps pile one atop another, not allowing a person time to recover from the last event, not only does depression take over, but it is accompanied by panic, fear, frustration, and indecision.

Born Mad takes you on a personal, in-depth account of my journey through thoughts of suicide and then fighting my way back from hopelessness, darkness, and despair. Also included are the therapies, techniques, and methods I tried in order to overcome depression, anxiety, and anger, with explanations as to what worked, what didn't work, and the reactions of my family and friends.

Having been diagnosed with this rarely talked-about form of depression, I'm telling my story to help you or your loved ones recognize the symptoms and seek treatment. Your life doesn't have to be filled with everyday worry, struggle, indecision, and bad choices. Help, happiness, and hope are possible.

Born Mad has three purposes. One is to chronicle the life of a person who, at one point, was unaware she had dysthymia. Hopefully the account of my anger and depression will help others struggling with the same thing. By comparing my life before and after my diagnosis, I hope *Born Mad* will help individuals realize they, too, might have anger and/or depression issues and seek professional help.

Two, I hope my account will help mental health professionals better understand anger and depression, so those with undiagnosed mood disorders and/or dysthymia will receive the treatment they need and deserve.

Three, I would like to create a dysthymia support group where people suffering from this little-known mental disorder can be diagnosed and treated earlier. In doing so, I hope to establish a charity that provides financial assistance for mental health assessment, follow up visits and prescription medication.

The names of my family, friends, coworkers, and counselors are not mentioned in *Born Mad*. They didn't ask me to omit this information, but I wanted to keep them anonymous for their privacy, as I did not ask for anyone's permission or approval to write my story. However, it is impossible to write about my journey without mentioning those with whom I interacted. So in turn, as a courtesy to those I have encountered over the years who might potentially want to remain anonymous, their names have been omitted.

While doing research about dysthymia, I found great sources of information, including books and journals written by psychologists and therapists discussing the causes of, symptoms of, and treatments for the condition. But I have not found a book written by someone who actually has dysthymia and suffers with its symptoms on a daily basis. (However, while in the middle of writing *Born Mad*, I found one book written by a woman who did suffer from dysthymia. Her book is listed in Related Resources under the Books and CD's section.)

I am not a therapist or a professional writer. I do not have a PhD in any area of expertise related to dysthymia, nor have I ever attempted to write a book before now. I do not consider myself an expert in anger, depression, or mood disorders. Simply put, I am one person who struggled for years to find answers to chronic, habitual anger and negative thought patterns and emotions. I wrote *Born Mad* in an attempt to bring attention to dysthymia so others can help themselves and the ones they love.

Not all anger is bad or harmful. Some anger can help release stress and can be a powerful motivator. Minor irritations about an event or a challenge in your life aren't necessarily bad, wrong, or shameful. However, when your anger lasts for days, weeks, or even months and you are unable to let go of it, preventing you from moving forward, it can become dangerous to yourself and others and will one day do more harm than good.

Born Mad is an "easy read." It is not cluttered with difficult technical terminology, nor does it include the kind of hard-to-understand subject matter you might find in a medical journal. Instead, *Born Mad* was written so every reader will find something of value in the examples and stories of my mishaps and poor judgment and so those struggling with anger, frustration, and dysthymic disorder will feel encouraged and hopeful.

Some parts of this book are joyful, but other parts are sad. I've emphasized the sad, angry, and unhappy events to point out how dysthymia distorts people's sense of reality and affects their everyday life. All these stories are real and truthful and have formed the person I am today. If one of these events had not happened, if one event or challenge had been different or omitted from my life, I would not be who and what I am today. They are the sum total of my life, and I am grateful for these experiences—even the moments of fear and despair—and what I learned from them.

Chapter 1
Born Mad

The waiting room was the perfect temperature, sparsely decorated with a few paintings and a large dish filled with hard candies. Soft jazz music was playing. The music calmed and comforted me, and I felt a little more relaxed and reassured. Even so, I was nervous and frightened to be in unfamiliar territory.

A small envelope with my name on it lay on the table. I reached for it and tore it opened. It was a note from the psychiatrist saying he'd be with me in a few minutes and to make myself comfortable. Those few minutes seemed like an hour, a dreadful, lonely, and agonizing hour.

While sitting in the doctor's office, all I could really do was pray. A few magazines were sitting on an end table, but I didn't feel like reading. Instead, I asked God for this to be the answer, the solution to my chronic anger, anxiety, and madness.

I had never visited a psychiatrist, so I had no idea what to expect. Would I have to give blood? Would the visit be physically painful? Would I know the answers to his questions? Was I manic? Did I have Obsessive Compulsive Disorder (OCD) or some kind of mood disorder? Was I really autistic, as neighbors during my childhood thought I was? This was the make-it-or-break-it point, the moment where I would sink or swim. My mind was racing with a million thoughts.

It may sound rather strange and morbid, but at this point, I wanted to be diagnosed with some kind of disorder. It was my last hope. I had tried everything I could think of—affirmations, anger management, the Emotional Freedom Technique, believing in God—but nothing had a permanent effect. I was still angry every minute of every day.

Was I really a mean, nasty, hateful person, or was my anger beyond my control? If my anger was due to a dysfunction, a chemical imbalance of some kind, then it wasn't *me.* I anticipated *that* problem could be treated with medication.

I sat in silence in the waiting room, still nervous but hoping I was mentally unstable, that I did in fact have a mental disorder. I am not a professional in the mental health field, so I didn't have the foggiest idea about what kind of mental disorder would cause chronic anger, but I hoped I had it—whatever it was.

During those few agonizing minutes sitting in the waiting room, I asked myself how I had gotten there. What events in my past had led me to a psychiatrist's office wondering if I had a mental disorder? Reflecting on the past events of my life, it all made sense. The last forty-four years of my life had all been leading up to this defining moment. This was the culmination, the sum total of my life.

* * * * * * *

Born on June 1, 1966, I weighed six pounds and four ounces, with a few strands of bright red hair standing straight up on my head.

Like most babies, I was born screaming at the top of my lungs. Little did I know this screaming would become a life-long pattern, haunting me for years afterward and leaving me feeling like I was always doing something wrong and the universe was out to get me.

My family consisted of my mother, my father, and my sister who was two years older than me. My father was a manufacturing engineer. Over the years, he had many interesting jobs, including assembling light bulbs and waterbeds. He was the prankster and jokester who gave my sister and I piggyback rides every night before he threw us down on the bed to "hit the hay." My mother worked at a retail store in the catalog pickup area, back when that kind of service was available. She was the one who brushed our hair and walked us to school; drove us to Girl Scout meetings, swimming lessons, and flute recitals; and read to us every night after dinner from the *Little House on the Prairie* book series.

No one knew I was born angry, although there were plenty of warning signs over the years. Plagued with sporadic episodes of anger as a child and into adulthood, I often frustrated my parents and sister, made more mistakes and blunders than I wish to admit, and messed up many parts of my life that I shouldn't have.

I learned that anger was a strong emotion of displeasure caused by some type of grievance, either real or perceived. Causes of anger, according to www.ezinearticles.com, include past experiences, behavior learned from others, a genetic predisposition, and a lack of problem-solving skills. In other words, anger is caused by a combination of two factors: an irrational perception of reality and a low frustration point.

These two factors were present in me even as a young child. I expressed my anger and frustration in various ways that should have been obvious clues to those around me that I needed help.

Cranky Baby

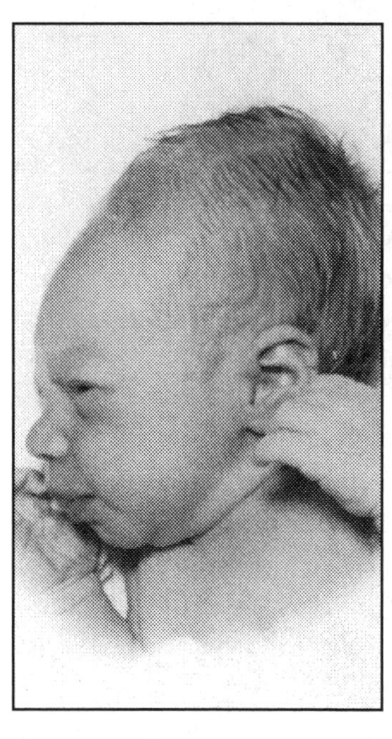

Intrigued by my behavior, my parents have told this story numerous times over the years. As a baby, I apparently disliked everyone, including my father. My mother and my grandmother were the only two adults who could hold me; no one else could get close. I would scream and yell at the top of my lungs, so no one dared come near me. My father couldn't hold me, feed me, change my diapers, look at me, or do anything that might involve coming within a foot of my personal space.

My aversion continued for a good six months. At this point, of course, no one will ever know why I acted like that. Since I can't explain what I was thinking or feeling back then and no one could read my mind, it will always be a mystery.

I do think my behavior was odd, even for an infant. One day, it appeared as though I just "got over it." My fits of rage stopped and suddenly I turned into a happy, bouncing, smiling baby—or at least that's what everyone thought.

I Lost My Kitty Kat

When I was one year old, I was given a stuffed animal—a cat with arms that had wire inside, allowing them to form a stiff circle so the toy could hang tightly around a bedpost or other object. It had a pink-and-white checkered body and fuzzy face, feet, and hands. I named it Kitty Kat.

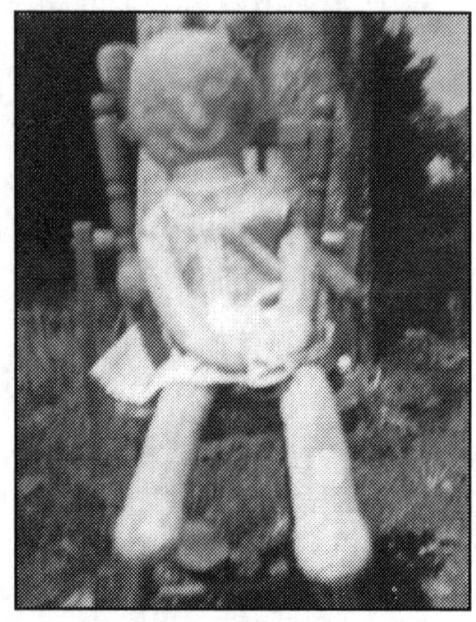

My sister got a green frog just like it. She put it on her bedpost, and it stayed there, nameless, looking brand new even years later. But not my Kitty Kat. I carried it around with me everywhere. I slept with it; I brought it to the dinner table, outside to play, and anywhere else I could think of.

Soon, Kitty Kat's arms were limp, unable to hang on the bedpost anymore. The fuzz on her face was gone, and my mother was forced to glue on new eyes, a nose, and a mouth because they had worn off too.

When I was two years old, I took Kitty Kat to my grandparents' house for the day. After a day of playing and running around, I joined my family as we all piled into the car late that night to make our way home. But about halfway home, I realized I had accidentally left Kitty Kat at my grandparents' house. Crying and screaming the rest of the way home, I made everyone miserable.

My mother begged my father to turn around to get my cat, but he refused. We were almost home; he was tired and wanted to put my sister and I to bed and call it a night. Still, I cried and begged. My mother put on my pajamas and tucked me in bed, but I still cried and screamed because I didn't have my Kitty Kat. I would not sleep and was determined that no one in the household would have peace until Kitty Kat was safely home again.

At ten o'clock that night, my mother and my grandmother met at a park halfway between their houses so my mother could retrieve my beloved Kitty Kat. After my mother arrived home, I snuggled Kitty Kat close to me under the covers and fell asleep.

Just Call Me Firebucket!

When I was about three years old, my godparents nicknamed me "Firebucket." Just by the sound of it, you know this can't be good, right? Well, it wasn't.

As a young child, my family frequently went to my godparents' house for dinner or the holidays. My godparents had four kids, all about the same age as my sister and I, and we liked to play together while the grown-ups chatted about the latest events and details of their lives.

One day, my sister and godsiblings ran out the front door to go to a neighbor's house. Of course, as is true of all small children at that age, I wanted to do everything the older kids did. But they considered me a nuisance, a tag-along little kid, so they sped out the front door so fast that it slammed closed in my face as they giggled and ran off.

My godparents lived in a large, two-story, five-bedroom home with extremely heavy double front doors. My parents said that I had, in the past, opened the doors by myself. This time I stood there screaming. My face turned red. I yelled at my folks, who were busy chatting. They could see me at the front door with my tiny fists tightly clenched, yelling at the top of my lungs.

I remember thinking I couldn't open the door, and I was upset that everyone had left without me. Being excluded and left behind was no fun. As a three-year-old, I didn't know what to do other than cry. My parents and my godparents continued with their conversation, taking a brief timeout to tell me to open the door and go outside.

After about five minutes of screaming, yelling, making fists, and stomping my feet on the ground until I was red-faced, my tantrum became entertaining for the grown-ups. My godfather said to my folks, "Wow, you got your hands full with this one!" Everyone laughed and joked that my face was bright red and thought if I could have blown fire from my mouth or nostrils, I would.

Again, my godfather piped up, saying, "She's just a small bucket of fire, isn't she?" And there it was, my nickname: Firebucket.

As I was growing up, every time my godparents greeted me or spoke about me, they called me Firebucket. Before that, they called me Robbie, which I wasn't really fond of, but I would have preferred that any day over Firebucket.

I am forty-four years old now. My godparents and I no longer live in the same town, and I haven't seen or spoken with them in several years. But I'll bet if we ran into one another tomorrow, I'd still be their little Firebucket.

I don't mind the name but rather how the name came about. I obviously had mood and anxiety issues, even at three years old. A small child having a temper tantrum over not being able to open a door and being left behind by the older kids probably needs compassion and comfort from an adult. Instead, I acquired a nickname that stuck with me forever.

Caution: I Bite!

At three to four years old, I started the awful habit of biting other kids. I bit kids in my preschool class, neighbors, friends, and, more than once, my sister. In fact, after a while, my sister recognized when I was going to bite her because I ran directly at her, full speed, with my little clenched fists waving in the air and my mouth wide open. She would scream, "Mom, this kid is gonna bite me again. Come get her!"

If other kids teased me, said things I didn't like, or just made me frustrated, I grabbed their arm and sank my teeth into their soft flesh like it was a big juicy hamburger. Have you ever been to the dentist to have a mold of your teeth made? A dentist would have had no problem making a mold of my teeth from the marks I left on other children. Many of those children were rushed to the emergency room so their bleeding wounds could be treated.

The next-door neighbors had three kids, and we played together frequently. But when I started biting them, their folks called my mother and told her she needed to take me to a shrink. They said maybe I had ADHD or autism or some other disorder, but my mother wouldn't hear of it. She would loudly protest, "Not my child! My child does not have autism! How dare you say that!"

One time, the neighbors forced me to go to the doctor with their son, who had blood trickling down his arm from the teeth marks I had left in his skin. To this day, I have no recollection of what the doctor said to me, but soon after that trip to the hospital, I stopped biting.

Today, knowing what I know now, I wish my mother had taken me to a shrink back then.

Shush… Listen…

My parents tape recorded one of my tantrums when I was about five years old. They claimed that I yelled, screamed, and snapped at people when I was asked a question. I, of course, angrily denied it, shouting, "No, I don't!" When the tape was played back to me, there it was: proof positive of my bad attitude.

After hearing my own tirades, my comments were somewhere along the lines of "so what?" My father told my mother I learned to snap and raise my voice from hearing her, that I was copying her behavior. Even to this day, most of my family members snap and raise their voices at others when asked a simple question. I don't believe any of us snap on purpose or to intentionally hurt other peoples' feelings, but rather we snap out of a knee-jerk reaction that became a bad habit early in our childhood.

* * * * * * *

At the time these events occurred, they meant nothing to me. I thought I was just being a child—and maybe I was. But today, knowing I have suffered from anger and anxiety-causing depression, most likely since childhood, I can't help but wonder whether these incidents were signs of my undiagnosed disorder.

Don't get me wrong; my childhood was not miserable. Good times and happy memories fill the spots in between the tantrums and fits of anger. One of my favorite memories involves startling a hospital orderly when I was four years old. I had been hospitalized for a few days to undergo tests for severe stomach pains.

One time, my parents showed up for their daily visit with a plastic snake that, when held by its tail, would sway back and forth like a real one. I enjoyed playing with the snake and couldn't put it down.

My prankster father had a plan and instructed me to stand up against the inside of the wall and wait for his cue. When he gave me the cue, I was to hold the snake outside the doorjamb just long enough for someone to believe it was a real snake. So when Dad gave the cue, I stuck the snake out the door into the hallway and then I heard it: a loud shriek and fast footsteps. As I peered out the doorway, I saw only a large clutter of towels piled on the floor.

My family was laughing hysterically, and I had no idea why. It turned out my father had waited until a female orderly with a fresh load of clean towels came down the hallway on her way to the linen closet. When she was just a few feet from the door, my father gave me the cue to put the snake in the hallway. The orderly, who turned out to be deathly afraid of snakes, screamed, threw her hands up in the air, and ran the other way. She then told the nurses and doctors that a wild dangerous snake was loose on the hospital floor.

Eventually, the hospital employees got wind of what really happened and, for the next three days, the hallway was empty. In fact, the crew flipped a coin to see who had the task of bringing the food tray to "the little red-headed girl's room."

And my sister and I used to drive my mother crazy at night. After my dad was worn out from the piggyback rides and Mom had tucked us in and turned off the lights, my sister and I would talk to each other from down the hallway. Our beds faced the same direction and, if we looked down the hall, we could see and talk to one another. We gabbed and giggled and laughed it up until my mother closed our doors and demanded we get some sleep.

Many more pleasant times filled my life, but when one suffers from dysthymia, the negative experiences prevail over the positive ones and dominate a person's thoughts. That is the nature of the beast and the theme of *Born Mad*.

Chapter 2
The Good, the Bad, and the Ugly

The psychiatrist's office was on the third floor, and the large windows offered a great view of the outdoors.

It was a breezy day, and the trees were peacefully and gently swaying back and forth. The large billowy oak trees reminded me of the large tree I could see from my bedroom window when I was growing up. My mind flooded with memories of my childhood. As I continued waiting for the assessment of my mental state, I reflected on my childhood and those fragile years of growing up and learning life's lessons.

My family and friends believed I was a happy child, despite my biting craze and tantrums. And as a child, I had no idea whether I was happy or unhappy. I was a kid; what did I know about how I was supposed to feel or act? I can say only that my happy and joyful memories of growing up far outweigh the unhappy ones.

My School-Age Years

Throughout my school-age years, I was constantly teased, harassed, and made fun of and was frequently the butt of practical jokes. My sister, schoolmates, and neighbors called me stupid, dumb, and ugly.

One of the many pranks my friends played on me was to pretend to eat grass and then laugh at me when I did eat it. After they pretended to devour several pieces of grass, saying, "It is so good and juicy. Try it, you'll like it," they dropped the small springs of grass on the porch when I wasn't looking. Not noticing the small pile of grass beneath their feet, I ate several pieces before they told me I'd been had.

And the day my sister and my next-door neighbors tied money to a string hanging from the garage rafters, I fell for that one, too. Stepping in a plastic kiddie pool to reach the money didn't tip me off and when I yanked on the dollar bill, a bucket of cold water dumped on my head. I was soaking wet from head to toe, and I ran home crying and screaming, ratting out my sister and my neighbors. They all got into trouble, called me a tattletale, and refused to play with me for days. But I was the only one who wasn't grounded for a week.

Then in sixth grade, I was invited to a slumber party at a friend's house. We were all lying in our sleeping bags, whispering about playing a prank on someone. Despite my insistence on knowing who the victim would be, no one would say, and I eventually fell asleep. When I woke up, I realized the prank had been on me. My so-called friends had crawled into my sleeping bag, stolen my bra, and frozen it overnight in a cup of water. I had to decide whether to wear an ice-cold bra or not wear one at all. My friends laughed hysterically and said the only reason I had been invited to the party was to be the butt of everyone's joke.

It is difficult, if not impossible, to grow up with healthy self-esteem or any self-confidence when you are the butt of everyone's jokes. Today, such actions are called bullying, and I'm glad to see kids and grown-ups speaking up about it. Back in the '70s, when I was growing up, cell phones, the Internet, Facebook, and texting did not exist. These things take bullying to a whole new level, and I consider myself fortunate the worst thing that happened to me was getting wet.

Stop Already!

After my parents married in their early twenties, they purchased a small house in a lower-middle-class neighborhood in Southern California. With one bathroom and three bedrooms, it was the third house from the corner on a busy street with lots of traffic. Our little abode was comfortable for a family of four. My older sister was born in 1964 and me in 1966.

My parents took my sister and I on yearly family vacations, but they came to a screeching halt when we were still very young. My parents argued a lot. It seemed to us like they never could get along or agree on anything, and neither would admit to having done something wrong. I used to think they argued about money, my sister and I, my dad's hobbies, work, and so on. But now as an adult, married and seeking a better outlook on life, I realized they just argued about who was right and who was wrong. Many nights I tried to fall asleep with the covers over my head, hoping to drown out the loud voices and yelling.

The neighbors would call, asking my folks to tone it down because the neighbors could hear the arguing from their house. When I invited friends over after school to play, to avoid the chaos, we ended up playing outside or they eventually chose to go home. And when my parents fought after my sister and I had gone to bed, we took turns crawling out of bed and stumbling into the living room to ask our folks to quiet down.

"Stop already," we pleaded. "We're scared and can't go to sleep."

My parents divorced when I was thirteen, but I wish they had divorced a lot sooner. But my grandparents convinced my mother to keep the family together "for the kids."

I'm not telling you about my parents' arguing and fighting to embarrass or insult them or hurt their feelings. I'm speaking up about it because, even today, I hear psychologists on talk shows and radio programs dishing out advice to married couples to stay together for their kids' sake. However, as a child of divorce, I much preferred shuttling back and forth between two houses than listening to the bickering. If two adults can't get along, it isn't healthy for their kids to witness this.

Watching two parents fight teaches children poor communication skills, scares children into believing their own marriages will be exactly the same, and leaves them with emotional scars for decades, if not for the rest of their lives. Living an in abusive household, whether the abuse is physical or verbal, is damaging to small children. If two adults can't get along, don't love each other, or have many years of built-up resentment and bitterness, children are better off with a split-custody situation than if they continue to witness the disconnect between their parients.

I can tell you, my parents' animosity toward one another affected me for many years afterward, especially after I married and had a spouse of my own. Kids are better off living between two houses, having peace and quiet, than living with parents who hate each other and are just trying to make it work for the sake of the kids.

Throughout my adult life, I've cowered when someone yells at me. Feeling like the little kid who hid under the covers when my parents were arguing, I backed down and failed to defend myself when others yelled at or chastised me. I've always hated the fact that I don't defend myself, that I don't stand up for what I want or think is best for me. I often get taken advantage of because I believe I have to do what is asked of me or I'm too afraid to say no.

Robyn Wheeler

Sisterhood

My sister and I were close when we were younger, as we loved to play and joke around together. We would record ourselves reenacting commercials, reciting word for word the advertisements we'd seen on television. We would jump rope, ride Big Wheels, and have, what we called séances with our friends at our slumber parties, although I'm sure they really weren't a séance per se.

To do this, we waited until late at night, turned off all the lights, and had one person lie flat on her back on the floor. The rest of us gathered around that person, and each of us put our index and middle fingers underneath her. When we tried to lift her up, she was too heavy; we could lift her off the floor only about an inch. When she was back flat on the floor again, we all chanted in unison, "Light as a feather, stiff as board, light as a feather, stiff as a board, light as a feather, stiff as a board."

After the third time, we again attempted to lift her off the floor using only those same two fingers beneath her. The idea of the ritual was to lift the girl off the floor as high as we could. Each time after chanting, we were able not only to lift her higher than the first attempt but eventually we lifted her so high we were able to stand beneath her. Then we would take turns being lifted until we all had a turn.

To me, this was the greatest thing. All evil spirits were gone, and we were one with the good spirits, becoming so light we were weightless. Back then, I could have told you exactly how it happened. But now that I'm in my forties, I can't explain it.

My sister was the pretty one with brunette hair, and I was the one with the bright orange hair and buck teeth. She was the straight-A student who excelled in music and sports. She won numerous awards for her flute playing, whereas I could barely get through one song without a wrong note or a mistake. We both played Bobby Sox softball. She made the all-star team every year, while I was an alternate one year out of three.

Our closeness as children changed drastically as we grew older, and anger and resentment took a foothold in our lives. We spent less time together and slowly grew apart.

After we both had moved away from home, my sister and I spoke on the phone frequently, but I never quite knew what to say to her. The mere mention of family events just brought out sarcasm and harsh judgment, as my sister hadn't spoken to many family members for decades because we didn't live up to her expectations.

When I moved to Texas, my sister called the state "the armpit of America," so talking about the cultural differences between the two states only revealed her attitude about how stupid and backwards she felt native Texans are. It seemed like the only safe topic of discussion was our jobs, but after a while, she accused me of wanting to talk only about myself.

My sister always seemed to be in the middle of a crisis or a predicament that she turned into something bigger and more dire than it really was—something that I do as well. When all was well, she talked and laughed and was her usual pleasant self. But when things went wrong, she responded to questions with one-word answers and palpable silence prevailed in between. Eventually our calls to each other were less frequent, and whenever we did communicate, it ended in disaster. She stopped speaking to me in 2008.

I've always loved my sister. At times, I didn't always like her but I always loved her. It wasn't until I chipped away my wall of denial that I realized she felt the same way about me.

Religion and Spirituality

Neither of my parents was religious. My family went to church until I was about four or five years old. I remember my parents' arguing about it but don't remember the specifics as to why they decided not to attend church anymore.

When my mother was growing up, she went to church every week but felt that God and religion were "shoved down her throat." When she wanted to go somewhere with friends, her parents either didn't allow her to go or didn't trust her to behave without supervision. She never wanted to force religion on her children, so nothing was ever discussed about God or spirituality after we stopped going to church. I basically grew up an as atheist; I did not believe in a higher power or that I was here on earth for a reason or a purpose.

That my parents did not include religion or spirituality in the lives of my sister and I is, in my opinion, one of the greatest mistakes they made. Growing up with no mention of our purpose here on earth leads to anarchy in our minds. We must come to realize that we are significant and were put on this planet for a reason. Without that awareness, life is meaningless, decisions are not taken seriously, and poor judgment prevails. And poor judgment leads to people waking up one day to realize they've made a chronic habit out of "screwing things up." On the other hand, when we realize that people are connected, that our decisions will eventually affect not only others in our lives but people around the globe for generations to come, we start thinking of the consequences before we take action.

Friends, coworkers, and others whom I encountered over the years talked to me about God. But after listening to them, I'd end up crying because I felt like I was doing something wrong or was upset because I didn't want to hear what they had to say. I felt worthless and inferior to those who believed in God or as if these people were trying to force their beliefs on me. Believing they were better than me because they knew God, I gave up and believed it was too late for me to change.

One of my best friends in junior high and high school was a Mormon girl who lived down the street from me. She was the most avid churchgoer I knew and never tried to push her beliefs on me or anyone else. I accompanied her to church a few times and didn't mind it, but either I never had the opportunity or the time to be diligent about making it a habit or I was just not interested in doing so. Still skeptical about a higher being who would pass judgment one day and brought floods, famine, and death to those who did not follow Him, I was not ready to put my faith in Him.

Today, this school friend and I live in Texas about an hour away from one another. She is an active, diligent mom who works from home, and I run my own business and have elderly family members to look after. But we still manage to squeeze in a quick lunch or a chat at her house every couple months.

In early 2009, Dr. Wayne Dyer's wonderful CDs about spirituality and inspiration convinced me to believe in God and that my life is working according to His divine plan, not the way I want or think it should be. I gave up all false beliefs that life "should" be the way I want it to be and surrendered to the fact that whatever is happening in my life is supposed to happen. God may not answer prayers exactly as they are expressed, but all is well and divine exactly as it is. God is all loving and all forgiving, and everyone is equal in His eyes of God. No one person is better or more important than anyone else. Everyone is special. (See Chapter 8, "No Coincidences.")

Old Family Patterns

Children begin learning behaviors and habits from their parents and caretakers at any early age. These behaviors, if positive, will help and benefit a child when he or she is trying to cope with dilemmas in adulthood.

Conversely, negative behaviors will only to detract and possibly cause harm to children when they reach adulthood.

My family was filled with jokesters and smart alecks who made a habit of saying things that were negative. The following are some of the sayings I remember or believed to be true, even when I reached adulthood. How many of them do you recognize or say on a regular basis?

"The grass is always greener on the other side."

"Let's not and say we did."

"You're only cute when you're sleeping."

"Do I look like I care?"

"If it weren't for bad luck, I wouldn't have any luck at all."

"I can't win for losing."

"Heaven doesn't want you, and hell doesn't care."

"Piss and bitch, moan and groan."

"Why do all the bad things happen to me?"

Rubbing a thumb and index finger together, asking, "Do you know what this is? The world's smallest violin."

"That sucks"

"That's stupid."

"It's a dog-eat-dog world."

"The one who has the most toys wins."

"Don't rush off thinking we're missing ya."

"Stupid is as stupid does"

"Don't let the door hit ya where God split ya."

By the time I was a teenager, I was an expert in sarcasm, insulting others and dishing out "zingers" with ease and no consideration for others' feelings. I hurt many friends throughout adulthood and didn't realize that sarcasm and criticism do not accomplish anything but serve only to detract from the current situation.

We all catch ourselves from time to time saying or thinking something that is negative. However, if you repeat and ruminate on all the negativity, you'll likely convince everything you've heard is true, and that may affect your state of mind.

At some time in your life, you will make poor decisions because you really do believe the grass is always greener on the other side and that if it weren't for bad luck, you wouldn't have any luck at all. These things eventually lead to bad attitudes and sour outlooks on life.

I was surrounded by people with the "irrational perception of reality" mentioned in the previous chapter. My family believes that every day should go as they plan, and everyone should be just like them. If they do not like a particular singer, food, or style of dress, then no one should.

In my family, we blame others for our anger. The actions of someone else are the reason we get angry. My family abounds with folks who have particular expectations of the world and the people around them. When things don't meet their expectations, they get mad, complain, and don't know to fix the situation.

The only truth in the world is what you believe. So you have a choice: You can believe all the negative thoughts and complain about them or you can believe positive thoughts that will benefit you and act accordingly. Pay attention to these thoughts and whenever you think negative ones, catch them and correct yourself before they go too far, before you really believe that "the one with the most toys wins." (See Chapter 8 for suggestions about how to change your negative attitude to one of prosperity and gratitude.)

Negative, self-defeating thoughts also create an attitude of entitlement. Have you ever met people who believe they are more special than you, that they are entitled to wealth, success, love, respect, or something else without having to earn it? People who hate seeing others have more money or possessions? People who believe that life is all about them and what they want, all the while failing to really see others around them? I'm sure you have because our society is filled with these people. Unfortunately, I was one of them for four decades. Read on to find out how I realized I needed an attitude adjustment and what contributed to my eventual enlightenment.

Next up … my unyielding denial of the truth.

Chapter 3
Unawareness

Sitting in the waiting room at the psychiatrist's office, listening to the jazz music, ruminating about how miserable I was, hating my life, and mere steps away from divorcing my husband, I could see denial was no longer an option. I looked back on my life, wondering why no one had told me about my bad attitude and everyday moodiness. Reality sank in, and I remembered various friends, bosses, and acquaintances who had tried to tell me I had an attitude problem, but I was relentless in my unyielding denial of the truth.

Denial, paraphrasing from *Merriam-Webster*, is the refusal to believe or accept; disowning or contradiction. Many people, including me, believe denial means failing to admit that you've done something even though you know you did it. Instead, denial should be referred to as unawareness. I wasn't dismissing something I believed to be true, because I didn't believe any of it to be true. I truly believed others were making things up.

Over the years, many friends, coworkers, and acquaintances told me I was angry, arrogant, and self-centered and had a bad attitude about life. My response would always be, "Yeah, right. There's nothing wrong with my attitude." One person even said, "If you think it's everybody else, it's probably you." I didn't understand then, but I do now. Boy, if only I had listened.

Being in denial about your attitude is similar to being a drug addict or an alcoholic. First, you have to admit you need help before you can seek it. No one can do that for you. You have to "bite the bullet," "tuck your tail between your legs," put your ego aside, and ask for professional help because you realize you are in too deep to help yourself. So even though many folks told me I had a problem, it took at least another twenty years for me to see it, admit it, dislike it (and myself), and seek professional help.

I honestly believe that all of us are born in denial. It takes a catastrophe of some form to wake us up so we find inspiration and enlightenment. We all suffer tragedies, setbacks, or illness. The issue is not *if* these things happen but *when* they will happen to us.

Here are a few stories of my deep, unyielding denial of the truth.

No Trading Places

While growing up in Southern California, my family lived next door to a young man who was a gifted and talented gymnast preparing for the Olympics. In the early '70s, a terrible trampoline accident rendered him a paraplegic. Being a child when the accident happened, I didn't really have any lengthy conversations with him until I was in high school.

This neighbor, after talking with me for a while, told me he would never change places with me even if it meant he could walk again. He said I was negative, emotionally unstable, and moody and those things would make my life miserable. He said he'd rather be happy with a positive attitude and never walk again than trade places with me. Of course, I didn't understand. Who in their right mind would not do anything they could in order to walk again, even with a bad attitude? I looked at him, pitied him, and swore I would never live in a wheelchair, no matter what!

Today, however, I understand what he was telling me. With a positive attitude, even not walking again is tolerable. Thousands of people live in wheelchairs and lead happy, productive lives. Some write books or became public speakers. Some go on to enter the Special Olympics. And those who have lost a leg (or even both legs) due to an injury get a prosthetic leg that enables them to walk and even run again. Attitude is everything, and mine was leading me on a downhill path, not an uplifting, inspiring one.

I'm Staying as Far Away from You As I Can

A few years later, when I was in college, I met a really nice guy. I don't remember his name, but he was cute and fun, and I wanted to go out with him.

One day, we stood in one of the parking lots and talked for nearly an hour. I don't remember the details or what we spoke about, but I remember his answer when I asked him when we were going out. Bluntly, he replied, "Never. I'm staying as far away from you as I can." I was absolutely blown away. I thought we were getting along and things were going well.

"You are extremely neurotic and need to live in the moment instead of in the past," he explained. "Get rid of your resentment and start going to church so you can become a better person. You are extremely opinionated, and eventually it will all catch up to you. Maybe not until you are in your forties and are told you have diabetes or someone in your family dies, but later on in life, you'll have big problems. You are no one I want to settle down and raise a family with."

The nerve of him to say that about me. He obviously did not know what he was talking about. Oh, well. Who needs him anyway? I laughed as I drove away. I never saw him again.

Twenty years later, I saw his predictions were correct in every way, from the diabetes diagnosis to my age and caring for family members. I'd say this was a huge coincidence, but since I do not believe in coincidences, I can only believe it was an act of God. It was meant to happen, and I was meant to remember it twenty years later. (See Chapter 4, "Better Off Dead.")

Bad Reviews

In my early twenties, I landed a job at Disneyland's Circle D Corral taking care of their livestock, including horses, cows, and goats. The stable area was on five acres, backstage, where guests aren't allowed to go. The department was small, consisting of about thirty-five other cast members and about twenty draft horses, along with other livestock.

It was the best job ever. I got paid to wash horses and ride or walk them in the park's parades—generally "horsing around" all day long. I loved the work, most of the people, and the company in general. But every year, my performance review would be all over the place. In categories related to job knowledge and the quantity and quality of work, I excelled, usually receiving above-average marks. But when it came to getting along with others and public relations, the reviews were negative. Words like "moody," "unapproachable," "always mad," and "complains" were used to describe me.

Every year, I angrily signed my review, stormed out of the office, and complained for days about how I was being railroaded and my bosses just didn't like me and wanted revenge. Other coworkers would tell me that I lived in my own little world. Not knowing or caring what that meant, I went on with life and, year after year, never understood why my reviews said I was mean, cranky, and moody. Twenty years later, I understand just how right they were.

I often wonder why I had any friends. I couldn't have been fun to be around. I wasn't someone *I* wanted to be around, so how could I expect others to want to be around me? The few friends I had would come and go once they realized what I was really like.

For someone like me, with dysthymia, life was great when everything went according to plan. But when life didn't go according to plan, I became irritable and difficult to be around, so people backed away and left me alone. Then I wondered why my friends weren't my friends anymore. I was not included in parties or events and then when I found out about everyone was invited except me, I stormed off in a fit of rage again. It never occurred to me that my reaction was the very reason I wasn't invited.

Death of a Relationship

In the '90s, I started dating a great guy. He was fun, cute, and someone I could see myself with in the future. We went on a few dates, but I embarrassed myself after the first time he stayed the night and things ended after that.

I hadn't heard from him for about a week. I was upset that he would stay the night and then not call to ask me out again, so I decided to call him. But when I called, I didn't leave a nice message like, "Hey, had a great time when we went out. Hope you're doing well, and hope to see you again. Call me when you a chance." Instead, I jumped to conclusions, not knowing the full story, and left a nasty, bitter, though unrehearsed, message. I never rehearsed the nasty message in my head, but when I heard the beep to leave a message, I said something like this: "I don't like guys who sleep with me and don't call afterwards. I'm mad and think very little of someone who would do that kind of thing."

About two days later, he called back, explaining that his cousin had been in a motorcycle accident, and he had been out of town attending the funeral. Boy, did I feel like an idiot. That angry, judgmental phone call cost me a great relationship. Still, it would be years before I figured out what caused me to react the way I did.

Family Genetics

My sister, when we were still on speaking terms, tried telling me about our family's attitute problem, but I wouldn't listen.

My sister had quit talking to my mother years before, claiming my mother could be mean and her moods changed many times on a daily basis or just over simple conversations at the dinner table. Again, I denied it, defending both my mother and my grandmother, claiming they were sweet and nice and so was I. Insisting she was the one with the problem, I told my sister she had the right to feel how she did, but she was wrong. How could many members of the same family have the same problem? To me, this notion was inconceivable. Of course, I was young, in my 20's and thought I knew everything. Little did I know until I was in my forties that some forms of mood disorders and depression are indeed, inherited and therefore a genetic factor.

What a Dork!

Single throughout my twenties, I lived in a two bedroom apartment and depended on roommates to help me pay rent. The roommate I remember most was a taxicab driver who worked nights and, ironically, didn't have a car, so he rode the bus everywhere. He told me he loved his job, never got mad about anything, and spent most of his leisure time in his room listening to tapes and CDs.

A few days after he moved in, he posted signs all over the house, signs that said "Make it a good day" and "Positive mental attitude." He had printed them out on a computer, laminating each one so they all looked nice and professional, and then tacked them up on the bathroom mirror, the doors and walls, and in the kitchen. I thought he was a dork. What kind of person needs someone to tell them to think positive? To me, it was just strange.

Eventually, he offered to let me listen to some of his positive-thinking tapes, including ones by Norman Vincent Peale and Dr. Wayne Dyer. But I'd be damned if I was going to do that! I had better things to do and, besides, I didn't need them. Those tapes were for dorks.

During the two years we were roommates, I thought my roommate was a lower-class citizen because he drove a taxi and rode the bus. I didn't perceive either one of those things as glamorous or ambitious, so I didn't believe anyone could be happy being a taxi driver and not owning a car.

He eventually moved out for reasons I don't remember, but what I do remember, even to this day, is that I never once saw him get mad or raise his voice in those two years. He never complained or criticized other people; he loved his life and enjoyed every minute. He was easygoing, went along with whatever someone else wanted to do, and always seemed to be in good mood. I thought he was a total nerd and a weirdo! I'd never met anyone who didn't get mad or have a strong opinion about something or endure daily difficulties. It seemed as though nothing bothered this guy. He just took what came along, never complained about anything, and seemed to cope easily with whatever came his way. Was he a robot or an alien from outer space inside a human's body? Did he have a secret or special tool that no one else knew about?

Little did I know that one day I'd be the same "dork," listening to positive-thinking tapes, revering Dr. Wayne Dyer, and posting affirmations on my bathroom mirror, the doors, and my refrigerator—all in an attempt to feel happy, be in a good mood consistently, and cope with whatever came my way. I wonder what my life would have been like had I just tried listening to one of tapes back then.

To Surf or Not to Surf

In April 2005, my sister wanted to take surfing lessons for her birthday. She sent out an e-mail to her family and friends, asking if we would all pitch in a few bucks, as she didn't have quite enough money. She already owed me a few hundred dollars, and every time I spoke to her, she was broke or struggling with finances.

She'd never mentioned wanting to learn to surf before, even though we grew up just miles from the beach. It seemed like this surfing idea came out of the blue. (Now, I must admit, she probably had mentioned the idea and I just didn't remember, didn't think she was serious, or blew it off because I didn't want to learn to surf.) Adamantly refusing to send her any money, instead I probably sent her a birthday present she really didn't want or need.

About a month later, my sister and I got in an argument, and she said I was the only friend or family member who didn't chip in for her surfing lessons. At the time, I didn't realize how judgmental I had been and didn't think she deserved to do anything "fun" since she still owed me money.

In 2008, when I came across the work of psychic Sylvia Browne, I knew I had been wrong. She says it is inhumane and cruel to stifle someone else's growth. By not chipping in and encouraging my sister to try something new and different, I stifled her growth as a person. It took my two-year journey of depression and anger for me to realize just how wrong I really had been.

Judgment Day

In the summer of 2005, my sister and I were communicating by instant messaging when she mentioned she was dating a new person. She was happy and excited about meeting someone new, and all I did was insult her. I implied that I wasn't happy for her because she'd probably break up with this person within two years and would look for someone else. I was sure her relationship would fail.

Angry about my judgment and criticism, as she had every right to be, she signed off instant messaging in a hurry. Another month or two probably passed before we spoke again. Still, I didn't get it. Instead of being encouraging, uplifting, and happy for her, I thought I was right in making judgments, putting her down, and telling her how to live her life. I was, of course, wrong again!

Happy Easter! Happy Easter! Happy Easter!

Before describing the most challenging event in my life, at least up to that point, I need to add that, after numerous failed relationships, I married in 1998. My husband is twenty-eight years older than I am and has three grown children and four grandchildren. We met when I began working as an animal control officer for the City of Orange in California, and we married two years later.

In August 2005, my allergist informed me I needed to undergo a procedure to clean out my clogged sinus cavities, remove a large wart on my uvula (the small piece of flesh hanging in the back of the throat), and remove my tonsils. Terrified at the idea of being put under anesthesia, I fell apart. After four years of allergy shots, numerous bouts of tonsillitis, and a wart that started out as the size of a pea when I was thirteen but had grown to the size of a grape, making swallowing difficult, my health would not improve without surgery.

My husband's birthday was the day before my surgery. I sulked all day, talked to my sister and my mother, and felt like I was saying good-bye to everyone. I cried most of the day, and it was the first year that we didn't celebrate my husband's birthday. We stayed home all day while I cried and threatened to back out of having surgery.

I was convinced something bad would happen during my surgery and I would be scarred or even die, but my husband tried to calm me down and talk some sense into me. But inside, I was angry and depressed and felt like my life was being turned upside down. I became immobilized with fear. Today, I look back on this and wish my family had realized how neurotic I was and insisted I see a therapist. But no one thought I had a problem with neurosis, fear, or anger.

Early the next morning, my husband drove my mother and I to the outpatient center about an hour away from my home. While sitting in the waiting room at 6 a.m., I cried until I couldn't cry anymore, begging my husband not to make me have surgery. I screamed, fought, and argued, pleading with anyone who would listen to take me home. At one point, my husband actually did offer to take me home.

But I knew surgery was my only hope. For years, my sinuses had been clogged with old, hardened mucus, and it was becoming impossible for me to clear my passageways when I had an allergy attack. Stuffed up all night and all day, forced to breathe through my mouth, I had numerous coughing attacks due to a dry throat, and no medication on the shelves seemed to alleviate the problem.

So I hesitantly stayed, following the nurse down the short hallway to the dressing room, where she instructed me to take off my clothes and jewelry, put on the gown, and wait for her to take me to a bed. Once in the bed, my mother and my husband were allowed to keep me company, and I was crankier than ever before.

A small child, most likely an infant or a toddler, kept crying on the other side of the curtain. She was obviously scared, too, and needed comfort from her parents. She had some kind of toy to help keep her calm, which kept repeating "Happy Easter! Happy Easter! Happy Easter!" After about five minutes of listening to this child cry and yell, I bitterly remarked, "Just one more happy customer, huh?" And I don't believe you really want to know what I threatened to do with the toy!

Eventually, the anesthesiologist came in and spoke to me, and I responded in a bitter and mean tone. I told him to make sure they removed my uvula and not the female body part that's spelled similarly. He injected me with some cocktail and in about a minute, I was feeling good, laughing and joking. When the stretcher pulled away, taking me down the hallway to the surgery room, I commented about needing an "E ticket" to get on the ride (a Disney reference from when individual tickets were distributed for particular rides instead of one all-day pass good for all attractions).

The surgery took more than an hour, but it seemed like a minute to me. I woke up with cotton stuck up both nostrils and a nurse forcing crushed ice down my throat. I remember constantly pushing her hand away because, when I closed my mouth to swallow the ice, I couldn't breathe. I kept refusing the ice, and she kept insisting I swallow it.

My mother assisted the nurse in putting me back into my street clothes, and I was wheeled out to the car. I could hear my husband and my mother conversing, and I wanted to talk but couldn't get any words out. They laughed on the drive home about me being so quiet and subdued. Those were the first moments of peace either one of them had enjoyed in several days. To this day, they both claim they will never forget that ride home and the "Happy Easter" toy.

Help! Anybody?

In September 2005, my entire family and two friends got together for my stepfather's birthday. He had been diagnosed with prostate cancer, which had spread to his lymph nodes. Before my folks arrived for the celebration, a friend said she didn't think he would live another six months. Sitting next to us was his teenage granddaughter, who was instructed by my friend to not repeat what had been said.

I had to admit that I agreed with her. By the way his condition was accelerating and the way he was acting and showing signs of deterioration, most friends and family were not optimistic about his lasting even another year.

At dinner, along with my family, were my stepfather's two daughters and a few of his grandchildren. As with most of our family dinners, we gathered at my grandmother's house and my mother, my grandmother, and I cooked, cleaned up afterward, and attended to all the other tasks that needed to be done to feed such a large crowd.

After my stepfather's side of the family left (they were usually the last to arrive and the first to leave), my mother started complaining about his kids not helping out. They rarely brought food to such functions or helped set the table, and they usually left prior to the cleanup. And both girls always seemed to make a big plate of leftovers to take home with them.

I didn't disagree with my mother. But instead of saying something or asking the girls to help out, she waited until they were gone and complained to the helpful members of the family about the lack of assistance.

My stepfather phoned the next day to ask whether our friend had said she didn't think he'd live another six months. Obviously, his granddaughter was extremely upset by the comment and told her mother about it.

I told him it was true and then proceeded to ask him why his children refused to be helpful, repeating verbatim what my mother had said about his kids. I called them lazy and fat and said I was angry they made my ninety-year-old grandmother do all the work and never even asked if they could do anything to help.

Unknown to me, both his daughters were at his house at the time and were able to hear every word through the phone, so that was the end of that. His daughters thought I was being mean and had no right to complain, and they never spoke to me again. I called, e-mailed, and repeatedly begged to discuss what happened so we could talk and work things out, but I never received a reply. One of my step sisters at the time owed me several hundred dollars. Because of my rudeness she stopped sending payments and I was never paid back for the loan.

My stepsisters and I were never close; we associated with one another only at family gatherings. They've moved out of state, and no one on my mother's side of the family hears from them. My stepfather did indeed pass away six months after that incident, in March 2006.

* * * * * * *

My journey out of denial was slow and gradual. It took years of events, thoughts, and feelings to lead me to awareness. However, when it hit me, it hit me hard, unexpectedly, like a brick had fallen on top of my head.

I can't pinpoint an exact date or time when my journey out of denial started, but it was probably in late 2008 when I was contemplating suicide. It was as if my skull had been split open by that falling brick, and my brain released all the denial. It left my body like a spirit departing a corpse, and I was stuck with nothing but unhappiness, disorder, pain, and loneliness, sure that no one would understand.

Denial is like an eleven-foot brick wall standing between you and awareness. You can't see over. You can't see around it. In order to expose the world on the other side the brick wall has to be knocked down. And only the person who constructed the brick wall can destroy it. My brick wall took over forty years to slowly and gradually erode and fall apart. Once the wall was in pieces, I was free to see the beautiful world on the other side—a world I'd never knew existed.

I understand why people don't come out of denial. Denial is safe, familiar, and comfortable, and it doesn't require you to do anything. At the exact time I realized my denial had lifted, I wished I had stayed in denial. The first glimpses of awareness and enlightenment were scary and intimidating, like a huge flesh-eating monster had been set free to consume "the old me." I felt like a small child lost in the wilderness asking, "What do I do now? What direction do I go? How do I get to the other side?"

Emerging from denial was mentally and emotionally painful. It was awkward and frightening, and I felt out of control. At the same time, I knew I would never be in a state of denial again—it just wasn't possible anymore—but I wanted to go back anyway.

After the first few days of ditching denial, my first thought was that I should apologize to everyone I had ever met. I felt embarrassed and ashamed that I hadn't realized my depression, anger, and mood disorder many years ago. No one could or would ever understand what it feels like. More helplessness and worthlessness sunk in as I realized I couldn't go back to apologize to 90 percent of the people I had hurt. All I could do was look to the future, find a cure for my anger, and do better next time.

Please don't believe for one minute that I told you my stories of childhood tantrums and adult denial because I am proud of them. In fact, the exact opposite is true. I'm conveying these stories in the hopes of helping others who may be behaving in a similar fashion and don't realize why. These stories are the "worst" of being me. Remembering these stories and writing them down for others to read left me with overwhelming feelings of guilt, shame, and embarrassment for a long time afterward. It took years until I was able to put them behind me, learn a lesson, forgive myself, and move on with my life.

Chapter 4
Better Off Dead

Finally, the time had come. The psychiatrist called me into his office, sat down in a chair across from me, and asked me why I was there. After explaining my chronic feelings of anger, resentment, worthlessness, and general uneasiness about being me, I added the events of the last eighteen months of my life that had contributed to my sadness, depression, and not wanting to live anymore.

Even though I had been angry and depressed on and off for years, I never thought of suicide until I was in my early forties and became bogged down by physical illnesses and a few unfortunate events that I didn't know how to cope with.

Beginning in May 2007, my undiagnosed dysthymia became more severe, and I plummeted into despair. I was angry and upset every day. All the negative events in my life became exaggerated, consuming my thoughts. The positive aspects of my life slowly melted away, becoming a distant past I barely remembered. My depression, fear, and anxiety were all compounded by the fact I didn't know how to cope.

As the psychiatrist took out a thick pad of lined yellow paper and began to take notes, I wondered if he could really help. I told the psychiatrist about the events that brought me to suicidal thoughts, seeking out professional counseling, and hating my life. My nerves were calmed and quickly dissipated with his soft-spoken voice and quiet, caring demeanor. No blood or urine test or MRI can diagnose depression or mood disorders. Knowing my answers were essential, even critical, I laid everything on the table and gave only honest and real answers that would hopefully lead to a correct diagnosis.

Please keep in mind a few things when reading about my journey. First, these things are not the worst anyone can go through. They are not life-or-death situations. There are people in the world who go through much worse. I'm not telling you my story because I want sympathy and think I've suffered more than anyone else in the world. I'm simply writing about my experiences and my thoughts about them, so if you, too, are going through similar situations, you might benefit from reading about what happened to me.

Second, at the time these events took place, I did not know I was suffering from depression or a mood disorder. Being unaware of this only caused intense fear, anger, frustration, anxiety, an inability to make decisions, and often a tendency to exaggerate the events in my life—to "make a mountain out of a molehill."

Atrophic What?

In mid-2006, my husband and I started taking turns helping my mother care for my ninety-year-old grandmother. She was showing signs of dementia and needed to be monitored much more than she had in the past. She was starting to forget names, making toast in the microwave instead of the toaster, answering the phone with the TV remote, and putting the TV remote in the phone charger.

My husband and I would prepare dinner after I got home from work, stay with my grandmother until my mother came home from work around 8 or 9 p.m., and then do it all over again the next day. In the year and half that my husband and I helped care for my grandmother and juggled our business and personal life, my health took a turn for the worse.

In May 2007, my first minor illness occured. A thick, goopy mucus started coming out of my eyes, and they itched like mad and were bright red and very painful. After a visit to the eye doctor on one of my few days off, I was given a bottle of drops to be administered six times a day for a bacterial eye infection. It cleared up after about two weeks—or at least I thought it had cleared up.

In July 2007, a visit to my general practioner was necessary due to the itching, dryness, and pain I was having in my "female area." After using Depo-Provera (injectable birth control) for four years, the shots had depleted my estrogen to the low levels commonly seen in menopausal women. My general practitioner had allowed me to stay on the injectable birth control two years longer than recommended. She was unable to determine what was causing my symptoms, so I found a new doctor, a certified gynecologist, who knew exactly what was ailing me. Atrophic vaginitis was the diagnosis, but I had never heard of it.

Atrophy, paraphrasing from *Merriam-Webster*, means a wasting away of body tissue; the failure of an organ or part to grow or develop. The suffix "itis" means inflammation. So, to put it bluntly, my vagina was dying, swollen, and itchy. My new gynecologist immediately discontinued the Depo-Provera shots, scheduled me for a bone density scan, and sent me home with a tube of Premarin, an estrogen cream, to relieve my itching and restore my body's estrogen level.

Before explaining my estrogen allergy, I must explain about the itching in detail. Have you ever had an itch you couldn't scratch, say on the bottom of your foot after you've already put on your shoes and socks or in the middle of your back where it was just out of reach? Drives you crazy after a while, right?

Atrophic vaginitis is an intense, unreachable itch that lasts 24/7. It drives you to the brink of insanity, making you wish you could yell at the top of your lungs, jump up and down, and act like a loon. It goes to work and the grocery store with you, and it's with you at night while you are trying to fall asleep. All you can do is obsess about the itch because you can't scratch it. It's an itch that isn't appropriate to scratch in private or in public. And it's not even appropriate to use a backscratcher on (although I thought about it numerous times!). It's the kind of itch that would make an excellent method for torturing military prisoners, if someone could bottle it and sell it.

This may seem like "too much information," but let me explain my three reasons for such a graphic and crude description. First, I wrote it as a preview of what's to come for many women. According to the American Academy of Family Physicians (www.aafp.com) more than 40 percent of women are affected by atrophic vaginitis (also called urogenital atrophy). I had never heard of it before I was affected by it, so consider this my way of introducing you to another weird and seldom-talked-about disease. We women tend to view the vagina as a pleasure center, but when your estrogen level is almost nonexistent, that part of a woman's body will speak to you, loud and clear; you won't be able to ignore it, and it will not be pleasant.

Two, the intense itch that lasts for months on end with no relief contributed in a big way to my depression and thoughts of suicide. A woman who does not suffer from depression would be angry and "driven to drink" over this particular itch. A person with depression, even a mild form, would be prone to losing her mind. I felt as close to insane as I could get from the constant itch, day in and day out, with no relief. I spent many days on the phone with nurses and doctors, begging for a new medication or treatment that would control the itch. Literally and slowly, I was being driven crazy by an itch that could never be scratched!

And third, once I was prescribed a treatment, I soon realized I was allergic to it! Imagine months of dealing with an intense itch you are unable to scratch and then finding a treatment only to discover the side effects are worse than the itch was in the first place. Wouldn't you be overwhelmed with rage, frustration, and anxiety? I sure was, enough to believe that being dead was better than my current situation.

Estrogen Allergy

Allergies are common for me—from pollen, dust, and perfume to cheap metals like nickel (often found on the backs of watches). With red hair and a fair complexion, my skin tends to be more sensitive than most people's. When my skin is irritated, red welts develop and my skin starts to peel off. However, what happened next was enough to make me feel like a freak.

A week after I began using Premarin, red welts appeared on my legs. Looking similar to bug bites, I ignored the welts for a few days. But as the days passed, the welts increased in size and spread from both knees up to my torso. At first, it looked like I had poison ivy. The welts itched intensely, caused extreme pain at the slightest touch, and were constantly oozing fluid. I waited several weeks for my next doctor's appointment, in the interim rubbing every over-the-counter cream and gel I could find on every inch of my legs.

Lying on the living room floor with few clothes on, I cranked the ceiling fan on high and hoped nothing and no one would touch me. I lay motionless, as tossing and turning would only cause pain to my cracked and itchy skin. I normally dislike being cold, but the cool air made the itching, swelling, and pain seem to ease a little.

Finally, my appointment rolled around, and I was told the welts were a severe allergic reaction to estrogen. But how could that be? How could a woman be allergic to a naturally occurring hormone in her body? What woman is allergic to that? I felt like a freak. I sat in my mother's car, crying and screaming at her: "Why did you give birth to me in the first place? How could you want a child who is a misfit, a freak, and a genetic mutation?"

How is it possible to be allergic to a substance that is essential to my existence as a woman? My mother was frustrated with my attitude and accusations and spent an enormous amount of time and energy attempting to convince me I was wrong, that I was neither a misfit nor a freak. But her powers of persuasion were not strong enough, and I firmly believed I was nothing short of a genetic mutation. I'd never heard of any woman being allergic to estrogen, so of course, I thought it was just me.[1] Like nothing ever goes right for me or ever swings in my favor. Whatever events that can make one's life difficult, frustrating and inconvenient will definitely happen to me.

During all this, the bacterial eye infection returned. So on top of a dry, itchy vagina, I had weepy, itchy eyes and legs. I felt like a hundred miles of bad road. I was depressed, didn't want to go anywhere or do anything, and was applying a medication for one thing or another every hour or two. Again, I was angry, and depression set in like never before. I felt I could not endure one more event or I would go crazy.

One Flat Tire, Two

A few days later, while traveling home from work, I saw another driver trying to get my attention. I pulled over to the side of the road and realized the left rear tire on my van was flat. The other driver who had gotten my attention was a young kid in his twenties, and he was nice enough to put the spare on my car. I then drove to the next town and pulled into a Wal-Mart to buy another tire.

In September 2007, I had another flat tire while driving home from work. This time, it was the right rear tire. Luckily, the Automobile Association of Texas had a tow truck nearby.

A flat is no big deal, right? It happens to everyone at one time or another. But please keep in mind a few things. One, I am a professional wildlife educator. I travel between fifty and one hundred twenty miles one way with as many as twenty-five live exotic animals. On any given day, I could be traveling with several dozen live animals, including small mammals; birds; reptiles; amphibians such as frogs and toads; and "creepy-crawly" animals such as spiders, roaches, and millipedes. All these animals are native to different climates and weather, so when I travel, my car has to remain at roughly seventy degrees to prevent any species of animal from getting too cold or too hot.

1 It is possible for some women to have allergic reactions to the main ingredient in Premarin, which is conjugated estrogen.

Me, as The Creature Teacher, with my two ball pythons, Rocky and Bullwinkle, giving a presentation at a local library.

Photo by Kerry Yancey. Reprinted with permission from The Monitor, July 21, 2002, page 3A.

In Texas, cool days are not a problem, but summertime is another story. When temperatures reach more than ninety degrees, the air conditioner must be on full blast at all times. If the car is not running, like when a flat tire has to been changed, the air isn't running either. Without fresh, cool air, my furry and cuddly friends like my rabbit, chinchilla, prairie dog, and hedgehog, can easily die in just a few minutes.

Two, although I had no idea I was suffering from dysthymia at the time, the flat tires brought out my inability to cope with unexpected events. People with dysthymia have a more difficult time handling normal, everyday mishaps than those who don't suffer from dysthymic disorder. People with dysthymia are happy when everything is going well; but when unexpected, unplanned events happen that are perceived as wrong, bad, or negative—even something as small and trivial as a flat tire, something most folks would be just slightly irritated over—a person with dysthymia sinks into fear, frustration, desperation, and panic.

These feelings lead to making poor decisions. A person cannot make a clear, focused, proper decision when feelings of inadequacy cloud his or her judgment.

Car Accident

In November 2007, I totaled my van in an accident that was entirely my fault. Tired and rushing to make a birthday party on time, I made a wrong turn. When I realized my error, I turned my van around and stopped at the stop sign. I looked left, a car was coming. I looked right, no cars. I looked left again, no cars. So I pulled into the middle of the two southbound lanes of traffic and smack, a small brown car slammed into the side of my van, caving in the sliding door.

After my van was pushed to the left so I was facing oncoming traffic, I pulled it onto a side street and checked on the driver of the brown car. We both sat on the curb in silence, waiting for the emergency vehicles to arrive. My van was drivable, but her car had to be towed.

I spent the next month feeling guilty, hating myself for not seeing that car. I sulked for days, mad at myself for panicking, speeding, and not paying attention. I couldn't smile or be happy or laugh. My husband tried to comfort me, saying our insurance company treated us well and assisted us in paying for a new and better car. But I didn't care about that. I was too focused on my huge mistake and unable to forgive myself.

Between the flat tires, my illnesses, and the accident, I once again wanted to crawl into a dark hole and not come out. Mentally, I beat myself up every day for making any mistake, even just one. The "tapes" playing in my head berated me over and over again. *Robyn, you are stupid, ugly, and fat. Everything you do is wrong; you're a failure and cannot do one thing correctly.* The tapes would not stop and, as they played over and over again, I cried constantly and didn't think I could get through another setback. But there was more to come, much more.

Internet Rip-Off

In February 2008, I purchased a corn snake on Reptimart.com from a man in Kentucky. This may sound a little strange, but as a wildlife educator, I frequently purchase animals off the Internet. I was creating a native Texas wildlife show and wanted to add a corn snake to my collection.

After sending a $160 money order in the mail, the man who owned the snake said he'd send the animal the next month when the Kentucky blizzard cleared up as the freezing weather would guarantee the arrival of a dead snake. But the blizzard cleared up and still my snake had not arrived.

In the next e-mail, the seller said he had been in the hospital with heart problems, but he would ship it out the next week. But the next month rolled around, along with the next one and the next one and the next one, and still I had not received my snake.

My husband offered to drive to Kentucky to pick up the snake, but this man was rude and had no intention of making good on his deal. We finally realized we'd been taken. My husband and I both took turns over those few months contacting various authorities and reporting the seller to the Department of Fish and Game, the Better Business Bureau, the owner of Reptimart.com, the sheriff's office in Kentucky, and the Internet Crime

Complaint Center. No one could or would help us. The sheriff's office in Kentucky visited his home twice but was unable to make contact with anyone at his known address.

To this day, I've never received the snake or a refund. Being the victim of Internet fraud is horrible. It's downright frustrating, maddening, and cruel. Dealing with this was more than I could handle. I wanted the seller to go to jail for the rest of his life and would keep trying to get him there until he got what he deserved. My festering anger didn't subside for at least a year. All the paperwork and proof of purchase was saved and filed so, in the event it became a court matter, I was prepared.

I cried and slammed doors for months after this incident, vowing never to forget that this man had stolen from me. Losing $160 dollars was not what really upset me; the money I could do without. But I hated being lied to and taken advantage of and, most of all, I wanted the thief to be punished. The fact that Internet crime is commonplace these days and the authorities, for the most part, have not caught up with current times was even more maddening. I knew I wasn't the only victim of this type of scam, and I couldn't understand why no one would help me get my money back. Today, I'm glad I was taken for only $160. I can't imagine how I would have reacted had I lost a few thousand dollars.

Death of a Skinny Pig

Also in February 2008, my skinny pig died during a break between shows. My allergies were bothering me; I was groggy from the Benadryl I had taken that morning; and I took a short nap in my car. I hadn't realized that this rare, unusual, and very expensive breed of hairless guinea pig had proceeded to chew off one of its feet while I was napping. By the time I found Brownie, he was cold and drifting off fast.

As someone who has adored and loved animals since childhood, losing a beloved pet is more than difficult, and I blamed myself for months. I should have checked on him and all the other animals that day. But I didn't, and coping with the guilt I felt was unbearable. Brownie didn't have to die, and I hated myself for letting it happen.

I arrived home extremely upset and wanted to close down my business. I felt like I was a failure at everything, even taking care of a small animal, so I did not feel worthy of owning forty exotic animals. My husband realized I was being a "drama queen" and blowing things out of proportion. He tried to tell me not to make a huge deal about it, but I wouldn't listen. I proceeded to yell at him for not caring enough about me, the animals, or the business and stormed off to turn in for the night.

Flat Tire #3

A few weeks later, I got my third flat tire in less than a year.

I was alone when I got the flat tire, driving home in the dark from a long day of birthday parties, and was forced to pull over on a very busy freeway. All I could think about was how it meant another bill and another hour of wasted time waiting for help—another crappy day!

Cursing aloud, I jumped out of the car, storming over to the passenger side to check the damage. A huge nail was embedded in the tire treads. I kicked the tire several times, using every curse word I could think of before calling for a tow truck.

Everyone deals with anger in different ways. Some people want to talk it out, while others remain quiet and withdrawn. I tend to do both. After I yell, slam doors, and make others miserable just because they're around, I get quiet. I don't talk to anyone about anything and go off to be alone, pouting and pitying myself.

After getting settled back in my car, I turned off the radio and had angry conversations with myself all the way home, going over and over in my head why the flat tire wasn't supposed to happen to me, how there was no reason for it other than just be another nuisance in my life.

When I got home, of course, my husband wanted to chat, and I wanted to retreat and be left alone. My husband endured a lot of days like that, the quiet ones where I wasn't in any mood to talk or share my feelings.

Mystery Side Pain

In April 2008, halfway home from another long day of birthday parties, I felt a nagging and excruciating pain in the side of my right breast, a pain that got stronger as time went on. I sped home, pulled into the garage, and bent over, crying while holding my side.

My husband transferred the animal crates from my van into the laundry room, gave me a baby aspirin, and then drove ten miles to the nearest emergency room. After a thorough examination, the doctors said I had bronchitis and pleurisy, wrote a few prescriptions, and sent me on my way.

After a routine checkup a few days later, I was notified by phone that my blood sugar was too high. The doctors were certain I had diabetes or some other type of endocrine problem, as well as low potassium levels and a failing gallbladder. Wow, a triple whammy!

Devastated by the news, I sank again into my self-pitying, negative attitude. I began the twice-daily ritual of testing my blood sugar levels and spent several days in the endocrinologist's lab giving blood for further testing. The thought of going through another surgery was too much for me. I was not going through that again because I wouldn't get through it. At this point, I truly believed I was better off dead.

After a battery of MRIs, CT scans, sonograms, and blood tests, the only problem that was confirmed was low potassium. The blood sugar test for diabetes was 5.9. (Anything over 7 means you may have diabetes.) My gallbladder and endocrine glands both checked out fine. But my side pain persisted. I visited several other doctors for second and third opinions but they both said it was a tweaked nerve and to take Advil every two hours until the pain went away.

Six months later, my pain subsided. To this day, no one, not even the doctors, knows what caused it.

Diabetes Phobia

Why was the idea of being diagnosed with diabetes so scary for me? Two reasons. First, my father was diagnosed with type 2 diabetes when I was a kid.

After my parents divorced, I spent weekends at my dad's so I could take horseback riding lessons. One day when my dad arrived to pick me up, my mother and I noticed he was talking strangely. He was slurring his words, winking at us, and not making much sense. Neither one of us knew at the time that his blood sugar was too low.

So off I went in a small sports car on a sixty-mile drive with my insulin-overloaded father. He barely stopped at traffic lights and stop signs; he changed lanes with no signal or warning to other drivers; and he sped up and then randomly slowed down over and over again.

We arrived at the stables safely but just barely. The stables were located at the bottom of a hill. A sharp turn into the driveway and then another sharp turn at the bottom of the hill were necessary to make it to the parking lot. My father just made the turn into the driveway but continued to drive straight instead, off to the right, down the driveway. He headed straight for the hill, hitting the brakes just in time to prevent us from driving off the hill into the parking lot.

All the trainers and riders heard the out-of-control driver and stopped what they were doing to watch the entire debacle. After my father successfully backed us off the hill and drove safely to the parking lot, one of the trainers escorted my father to the local ice cream stand for a soft-serve cone. I stayed behind and saddled up my horse for my lesson, and thirty minutes later, my dad came back acting like normal, with a sense of humor and an easygoing, laid-back attitude.

The rest of the weekend went fine. However, that car ride with my father scared the living daylights out of me, and whenever I hear the word diabetes today, I think of that day when I was almost driven off a cliff.

Over the years, I've heard friends and other folks talking about horrible things happening to people they know because of a bad reaction to insulin. In fact, in 2010, a family member lost his large boat parked in his driveway because an out-of-control diabetic driver ran over the curb and into his driveway and knocked the boat off its trailer. Family friends have told stories of their loved ones walking outside totally naked, not knowing where they were (or even that they *were* naked), or having limbs amputated due to years of diabetes. Diabetes runs on my father's side of the family. My great-grandmother and two great aunts were also dependant on twice-daily insulin shots, so I figured my chances of being a diabetic were pretty high.

The second reason I was concerned about diabetes had to do with my becoming a vegetarian in the early '90s. I didn't particularly care for beef or pork and decided once and for all, for the sake of my health and animal welfare, to be a strict vegetarian. Gradually, for fear of living a diabetic life, I began cutting down on carbohydrate-laden foods like beans, pasta and potatoes and began eating fish and poultry again.

Bird Feeder Fiasco

In May 2008, on day of my grandmother's ninety-seventh birthday, a large concrete bird feeder fell on my feet.

My husband and I had just parked at my grandmother's house and I needed something out of the side of the minivan. When I pushed the door open, a cement bird feeder that I was going to give to my mother fell on my legs and feet. Only wearing shorts and sandals at the time, I had little or no protection for my legs and feet. When the bird feeder fell, it severely bruised my feet and legs from my knees to my ankles.

Hardly able to walk, I limped to a chair on the patio and with a house filled with guests and relatives, started crying uncontrollably and telling everyone within range that I wished I was dead. I couldn't take it anymore. Between the illnesses, all the tests, the flat tires, the pain and agony, I was defeated. I couldn't fight any more. My willpower and mental strength were depleted. I felt beat down to nothing and wanted to give up. But despite my depression, my anger was raging out of control like never before.

My mother came out of the house and asked what was going on. I don't remember the exact conversation, but I do remember crying and saying I wanted to shoot myself, someone, anyone. I was convinced killing another person would make me feel relieved and less angry. If I could just take out my anger on someone or smash everything in sight with a baseball bat, I'd feel better, in control, and not so helpless.

Those terrible thoughts scared the living daylights out of me. Never before had I entertained such a horrible idea. Almost every night, the news is filled with violence—rape, robbery, murder—and disbelief invades everyone's mind, wondering how those kinds of things ever happen. Most people are sure they would never be capable of such violence. I was always one of those people, standing in judgment and condemnation of others who committed hideous crimes. But then, sitting on the chair on the patio, I understood the feeling. I understood the frustration, hurt, and mental anguish someone could feel that leads them to the point of wanting to harm another person.

When you're feeling overwhelming emotions of anger and worthlessness, that you can't do anything right or don't know how to fix any of your problems, thoughts you would otherwise never envision enter your mind. Extreme depression and aimlessness override common sense.

My mother cursed at me, claiming that someone was always ruining her parties. I yelled at her to go back inside. She did, and then I proceeded to run off the porch and down the street. My husband followed after me. I screamed at him to leave me alone, but he didn't. I hated that at the time, but later I was grateful that one person in my life was watching out for me.

Suddenly, I stopped running and stood in the middle of the street, crying and wondering why and how all these bad things were happening to me. What had I done to deserve such punishment? I worked hard, was faithful to my husband, cared for my elderly grandmother, and spent much of my free time with my family. Why was God punishing me? Why was my life crumbling out of control and I couldn't do a damned thing about it? Confused, afraid, and angry at God, my family, and everyone else in my life, I wondered what I should do next.

The fact that my mother showed absolutely no compassion toward me in this time of need was crushing. I needed to be comforted and held and told I was loved. Even if I did make a scene and didn't act the way she expected me to, I still needed compassion at that moment, not anger or blame. The one person who should have been worried and fearful that I really would kill myself cursed and turned her back on me. I felt her party was more important to her than I was. Devastated, confused, and already wanting to die, more than ever before, I wished I were dead.

Thoughts of Suicide

The mere idea of an insulin-induced reaction happening to me, especially out in the Texas country, driving around with a dozen or more live animals in my car, was too frightening to dwell on. Just the thought of getting into a car accident, hurting myself or other innocent drivers, was enough to make me consider closing my business for good.

I began crying in the middle of the night, telling my husband I wanted to die. I became immobilized with fear at the prospect of having diabetes and by May 2008, when the stress, worry, and anxiety were overwhelming and overrode any common sense or rational thought, I became suicidal. Truly believing I would be better off dead and unable to face any more illnesses, I had it all planned. I was going to swallow a bunch of pills while my husband was out playing golf. Or I was going to shoot myself, as we kept a pistol in a secret spot in the house for protection. Either way would work, as long as I found relief and could be mentally, emotionally, and physically pain free.

I remember just wanting my life back. How had everything gotten to this point? The weird thing about dysthymia is that most of the time, an individual is not immobilized by depression. It is so mild and rarely noticeable that most individuals are happy the majority of the time. But when the depression sinks in, it takes the person to the opposite end of the mood spectrum. In a matter of minutes, even seconds, a person can go from feeling happy and upbeat to being negative, pessimistic, and deeply depressed. A person with dysthymia allows one rotten moment out of a day to ruin the entire day. The many good, happy moments are ignored, allowing the one bad moment to overrule all the others.

I wanted the "happy me" back. I knew I would never be happy as a diabetic. In my mind, a diabetes diagnosis was a fate worse than death. It meant a life of agony, daily needle injections, and declining health.

Why didn't I kill myself? Many people say they don't go through with harming themselves because they think of a loved one, a pet, their job, or something they love to do that keeps them going. But for me, to be honest, I was too afraid to do it. I felt stuck, really stuck, trapped in a horrible hell I had no idea how to get out of.

What does a person do when she doesn't want to live anymore but is too much of a coward to follow through with her plan to commit suicide? Day after day, I tried to get up the courage, but when I came close, I couldn't do it. I wasn't afraid to leave my pets or my family behind. I wasn't afraid someone would find me and call 911 and I'd be hospitalized instead of dying. And I wasn't afraid to die. I was simply a coward; I lacked enough courage to go through with killing myself.

If you are considering suicide, please know there is a solution to your depression. You may not have dysthymia like me, but keep searching for the truth. Try everything out there that you have access to. Seek professional help and do whatever it is they tell you to do, but do not give up. Quitting for me was not an option. I had to rid myself of my anger before I hurt more friends and family—and myself—even more than I already had.

Unable to speak for others, I can only give you my account of wanting to commit suicide. I attribute my thoughts of suicide to truly believing I could not get through whatever hardships I faced. Feeling as if I was constantly sinking even though I know how to swim and drowning even though I was treading water with all my might, fatigue won, leaving me hollow inside.

Many people who survive the suicide of a family member ask, "How could he do that? What was he thinking? He had a family, a job. Didn't he think about what the suicide would do to everyone?"

Suicide is a selfish act. Contemplating taking your own life happens when you feel so overwhelmed by depression that no one else matters. When I was contemplating suicide, I didn't think of anyone else or how they would feel after I was gone. I only wanted to end my suffering, despite the pain it would cause my loved ones after I was gone. Their reactions to my death were not my concern at the time.

In the few moments that I did think of others' reactions, my thoughts of doom and dread only deepened and gave me one more thing I couldn't or didn't want to cope with. I couldn't think about the situation anymore; the more I thought about others, the more I wanted to die.

If you have had loved ones who killed themselves, they most likely weren't thinking of you or anybody else in their life when they died. Their mental capabilities at the moment would not allow it. They were able to think only of their inner pain and suffering, and not what you might feel once they were not around.

Surprise! Happy Birthday!

In August 2008, my husband turned seventy years old. My family and I gave him a surprise party at a fancy restaurant. His children and grandchildren flew in from out of state, and our plans went off without a hitch—until one phone call ruined the perfect day and my happy mood.

My mother called to say that authorities showed up at my grandmother's house, investigating a report of neglect regarding her care. I had been talking with my sister on the phone a few weeks before, explaining how upset I was that my grandmother was not in a nursing home. I was under a lot of stress, working too many hours, overwhelmed by my illnesses, and just frustrated with life in general. Feeling my grandmother would receive better care if she were in a facility, I was filled with anxiety and fear about the entire situation.

My mother, having power of attorney over my grandmother's affairs, was dead set on keeping my grandmother in her own home, even if it meant that other family members risked their own sanity, health, and happiness in order to achieve this. After listening to my complaints about seeing my grandmother in such a debilitated state, my sister was also angry and frustrated about the situation.

When I heard about the investigators showing up at my grandmother's house, I assumed my sister was behind the complaint of neglect. While my husband's children and grandchildren watched in disbelief, I frantically dialed my sister's number, she didn't answer. I couldn't ask her if she did, indeed, make the report but I left a mean, nasty message anyway. I swore at her using language I will not repeat here and told her never to call or write me again; I wanted nothing to do with her and never wanted to speak to her again.

In the following months, the investigators dropped by unannounced several times at my grandmother's house. They contacted friends, other family members, and acquaintances, drilling them about my grandmother's health, how she was being cared for, and how she was treated by those who were close to her every day. My mother was beyond dismayed, worried the authorities would rip my grandmother from the only home she had known for the past ten years and haul her away to be institutionalized. But when the investigators showed up, they always found my grandmother with plenty of food in the refrigerator, a clean and sanitary kitchen and bathroom, and many friends and family caring for her around the clock.

The neglect complaint was officially deemed unfounded, and eventually we could all go on with our lives as usual. Except me. I still had a few more blows and setbacks before life would return to "normal".

You Want to Biopsy My What?

Over the past year, I'd been back and forth to the gynecologist seeking treatment for yeast and bacterial infections that never seemed to go away. My "female parts" were still dry, itchy, and "driving me up the wall." (This was probably due to high blood sugar, as many women with diabetes or borderline diabetes have recurring yeast infections.)

In September 2008, no infections were discovered, so the doctor suggested a vulvar biopsy. Yes, ladies, a vulvar biopsy is exactly what it sounds like. With an instrument resembling a single-hole punch, the doctor removed a small piece of tissue from my vulva. The injection of a numbing agent was extremely painful, and the biopsy itself didn't feel much better. I was sore (and still itchy) for at least a month after the procedure.

When the results of the biopsy came back, I was relieved. Finally, the doctor could reach a diagnosis and provide a treatment for my condition so I could get back to a normal routine. The results showed that I had inflammation of the vulva. *Wow, really? I could have told the doctor that! Now what? Live with an itchy, dry vagina for the rest of my life? I don't think so!*

The atrophy disappeared a few months later—by shear accident, actually—when I started taking probiotics every day in an attempt to diminish occasional pains in my stomach. I had tried yogurt and acidophilus pills to no avail. Probiotic capsules have sixteen times the amount of bacteria compared with yogurt and acidophilus. With the addition of probiotics in my daily banana and strawberry smoothie (with protein powder, fiber, and fish oil as well), my female problems subsided within just a few weeks.

Back to the Emergency Room

Also in September, I woke up in the middle of the night with difficulty breathing. After my husband found me sitting on the sofa in the dark, gasping for air, he loaded me into the car in my pajamas and bathrobe and drove to the emergency room. Again, I was told I had bronchitis and pleurisy and was prescribed antibiotics. (*Oh, great; I can have yet another yeast infection*!)

Thankfully, this was the end of my pleurisy and my antibiotic regimen. Soon after, I slowly began regaining my health. However, I had to endure two more completely new and just-as-immobilizing health scares before my good health returned.

One Root Canal, Two

A few days after the biopsy and the second trip to the emergency room, I began experiencing sensitivity to cold water as well as pressure on the left side of my face. When I went to the dentist, he gave me two options: Remove one of my molars or have a root canal. I opted for the root canal, which took about an hour but couldn't be completed.

My husband had gone to run a few errands while I was in the dentist's chair and when he came back to the office, he found me sitting on the curb, crying at full capacity. The dentist was unable to complete the procedure on the last root, so he was sending me to a specialist for further surgery.

A week later, the endodontist removed a tiny sliver of metal instrument from the root of my tooth. He explained that it is not uncommon for instruments to fragment during surgery and fall into the tooth canal. That was the reason the dentist was unable to complete the procedure; he was completely unaware of what had happened.

November rolled around and I needed another root canal. Again, I began feeling painful sensations in the same area as the previous molar. Did the surgery not work? How was I feeling sensitivity in the same area all over again?

My dentist couldn't say for sure where the pain was stemming from and what the problem was exactly, so I made another trip to the endodontist to assess the situation. Sure enough, I needed another root canal in the molar next to the previous one. Again, my regular dentist performed the surgery but could not complete it. The next week, I went back to the endodontist for yet another surgery on the same tooth. This time, a fourth root was found as the obstruction and complication to the first attempt at repair.

The endodontist put fillings in both of my teeth but wouldn't put a cap on them, so after each root canal surgery, I went back to my regular dentist to have a mold of my tooth made. A few weeks later, I made another trip to the dentist to install and cement the crowns. Within two months, this was the tally: two dentists, two root canals, seven trips to a doctor's office, four of which required laughing gas and anesthesia, and a grand total of more than four thousand dollars worth of bills.

Granted, no one likes root canals, multiple trips to the dentist, or thousands of dollars spent on surgery. But for a person suffering from depression, the root canals just added insult to injury, so to speak. By this time, my mental, physical, and emotional energy was depleted, and my motivation to fight another day was dismal at best.

But I did live to fight another day, although I cannot tell you what kept me going, why I woke up every morning to face another miserable day.

Are You Serious?

In October, a month prior to the second root canal, I found a lump in my right breast while taking a shower. *Crap . Now I have breast cancer? I can't believe this!*

So it was necessary for me to go to yet another doctor to get a mammogram and a CT scan of my chest. I worried every day until the results came back. During that time, I was positive I had cancer and would suffer through numerous bouts of chemotherapy and eventually die. My thoughts of doom were normal for me, a person unknowingly suffering with a chronically depressive personality.

I was relieved and excited to learn the mammogram and CT scan showed the lump was just a cyst. Another surgery had been successfully diverted.

Angry E-mail

In December 2008, I hit an all-time low when I wrote a scathing two-page e-mail to a friend and competitor.

We'd been friends for about four years, e-mailing each other on interesting party mishaps, the projects we were working on, and general information that might assist each other in improving on our businesses and services. We were turning competition into cooperation, if you will.

But this December, I wasn't nice. My e-mail berated my friend for everything this person did that upset me. I accused my friend of stealing ideas, copying everything I did, and being hyper-competitive. My friend, unfortunately, received the brunt of my frustration, anger, and fear.

Many psychologists say the opposite of love is fear, and I believe it. When fear immobilizes you to the point where you cannot think clearly, make decisions, and ultimately function, it will turn you into someone you and others will not recognize, someone who doesn't consider others' feelings, only his or her own problems. Not only will you take out your anger on yourself, but you'll also turn it on the people you care about or have day-to-day contact with. My friends and family definitely received their fair share of wounds inflicted upon them by my ongoing rage and depression.

I had also changed the logo for my business and at the time should not have been making any major decisions. I hated the new logo; it wasn't what I wanted, but I thought it was "just one more thing that didn't go my way" and approved it anyway.

What I didn't realize until months later, when my friend e-mailed me stating we were no longer friends and I was asked to cease all communication,, was that my new logo closely resembled my friends business logo. The graphic artist who created my new logo had been hired less than a week before and therefore, he had not seen my friend's business logo before or even heard of this persons business. At the time, I was so worried and obsessed over the root canals, the possible breast cancer, and the diabetes scare that I didn't see the resemblance between the logos either.

Upon realizing the similarity, the graphic artist was more than willing to make a new logo for me. This time, I created all of it from the fonts, coloring, animal choice, and words. Down to the letter, the new logo was my creation so I longer had to worry it was similar to anyone elses.

It took me more than a year to realize we were both better off not being friends. During the next year, my blood boiled at not being able to give my side of the story. Until that point, I never really realized how much I was bothered by not being able to speak my mind and give my point of view.

My friend added insult to injury by not asking about my side of what happened, assuming my logo was just an attempt at imitating something I liked. The similar logo was a fluke, an accident, an oversight. I felt rejected, hated, and misunderstood. I hated having those feelings, letting someone's uninformed assumption dictate my thoughts and moods. That, in turn, increased my feelings of anger at myself and losing control. I've always valued my friendships and was proud that neither one of us got petty or greedy or jealous. The fact that I "blew it", handling the situation so immaturely and radically, made me realize I more than ever that something was wrong. I needed help or my thoughts would destroy me…and others.

Since going our separate ways, both our businesses have grown and gone in their own directions, and we don't mentally compete with one another anymore. It is said that when one person says good-bye both parties feel rejection. I'll never know how my friend coped with it, but in the end, we probably both believe everything worked out for the best.

Part Two

I Have What?

Chapter 5

Pot Brownies, Hypnosis, Lobotomy

After expressing my anger and hopelessness over my illnesses and my battle with my inner demons, the psychiatrist inquired as to the therapies I had tried to rid myself of hostile thoughts. I explained that over the past two years, I had tried everything I could think of, from meditating, praying, and dream analysis to palm and toe reading, affirmations, and anger management. None of them had the long-term permanent effect I was searching for. Here's my story.

One morning, in the middle of my eighteen-month journey of misery, I laid in bed wondering why my life wasn't working. I was unhappy, and though my illnesses were slowly being resolved, I still felt physically and emotionally worn out and as if everything was out of my control. I knew I needed help.

In a sudden moment of intuition, I realized I was angry at myself, others, and all the events that had transpired over the past year and a half. I'd been this way for a while. In fact, as I thought harder, it was difficult to recall a time when I wasn't mad. It had been years since I was really happy. Taking an anger management course seemed to be a good step in the right direction.

The Anger Test

While looking online for an anger management course, I stumbled upon a short quiz that ranks how quickly and easily an individual gets mad. Out of sixteen items, I checked off these twelve in the positive:

1. I become impatient easily when things do not go according to my plans.
2. I tend to have critical thoughts toward others who don't agree with my opinions.
3. When I am displeased with someone I may shut down communication or withdrawing completely.
4. I get annoyed easily when friends and family do not appear sensitive to my needs.
5. I feel frustrated when I see someone else having an "easier" time than me.
6. When talking about a controversial topic, the tone of my voice is likely to become louder and more assertive.
7. I can accept a person who admits his or her mistakes, but I get irritated easily at those who refuse to admit their weaknesses.
8. I do not easily forget when someone "does me wrong."
9. When someone confronts me with a misinformed opinion, I am thinking of my comeback even while they're speaking.
10. I struggle emotionally with the things in life that "aren't fair."
11. Although I realize that it may not be right, I sometimes blame others for my problems.
12. More often than not, I use sarcasm as a way of expressing humor.

Later, I found out the average score for the anger quiz is between six and eight. At twelve, I was way over the average. (You can find the Anger Test in *The Anger Workbook* by Dr. Les Carter and Dr. Frank Minirth.)

Beginning the Course

Being absolutely astounded by the number of items I checked off, I immediately signed up for an anger management course in the Dallas/Fort Worth area. I paid a small fee through PayPal and scheduled the first of four sessions.

In January 2009, I drove to the private home of a couple who admitted they had struggled with anger management themselves and now owned and operated their own business helping others manage their anger.

During the first few sessions, I met only with the female counselor and described the events of the past year and how they were affecting me, my family, and our lives.

The female counselor was very nice; she seemed quite intelligent and genuinely concerned about my situation. After revealing a little of her own background, she handed me a notebook with a few worksheets and information about how to identify positive and negative anger, the purpose of anger, and the effects of anger on others and on myself.

The most beneficial and life-altering information for me was in the section on self-angering thoughts. Many people have self-angering thoughts several times a day and do not realize how deleterious these thoughts can be on their psyche. I had many self-angering thoughts throughout my life, believing these thoughts were normal and everyone has them. See how many of these self-angering thoughts you have on a daily basis:

1. ***Labeling:*** This is using negative words and descriptions when referring to others. Examples: jerk, idiot, clown, doofus, buffoon, or any comments related to race or gender that would be considered a put-down or slander.
2. ***Mind reading:*** You know this one. It's when you are convinced you know something for sure without asking for a reason or the purpose behind the actions of another person. Examples: "He did that just to piss me off," "That was done on purpose," or "That person is trying to drive me crazy." Without ever asking, you assume you know the intentions of other person.
3. ***Fortune telling:*** I heard a lot of this in my family in statements like "I'm going to get fired," "I'll never have enough money to pay for that," and "I can't do that." This involves thoughts of knowing for certain what will happen in the future or deciding that since something happened in the past, it will definitely happen again.
4. ***Catastrophizing:*** My whole family does this—you know, when you exaggerate the importance of something that has happened. Instead of just being slightly annoyed or irritated about something, it becomes a matter of life or death. "It was horrible!" (awful, dreadful, unbearable, use your own adjective), or "That drives me crazy!" or "I can't stand that!"

5. ***"Should" Statements:*** These take something you prefer and turns them into demands, things that other people or you yourself "should" do. But that leads to an attitude that life is totally unfair and injustices are commonplace, as well as a self-righteous attitude. For instance, "He can't do that" or "She shouldn't have done that."
6. ***Vengeance:*** This involves thoughts of getting even and/or harming another person you think has wronged you. For instance, "I'd like to wring her neck!" or "I'm going to kill him!" or "Just wait until I get a hold of that kid!"

I realized that not only do I do all these things but so do most members of my family. Immediately, I typed up five items for my family to practice, if they were willing, at dinners, birthdays, and everyday visits. If I was going to change, I wanted support from my family in doing these things as well.

First, stop saying "I hate." Everyone in my family is big on this one, repeating it numerous times when talking about events, people, television shows, food ... just about everything.

Second, stop predicting the future. No one knows what will happen in the seconds, days, and months ahead, so there is no reason to panic or stress out over events that may or may not happen.

Third, avoid using words like "stupid," "crazy," or "wrong." Just because you don't understand why someone would pierce their nose or lip, go bungee jumping, or get a tattoo doesn't mean those things are stupid. It may not be something you would like to do, but that doesn't make it wrong or crazy for others to do it.

Fourth, avoid complaining. My family is big on this. Their behavior has always run along these lines: If you don't like it or think it's fair or right, then complain about it and expect the situation to improve just because you complained. Unfortunately, complaining accomplishes only one thing—it makes the "complainer" look bad, not the person or thing that is being complained about.

Fifth, avoid giving your opinion if it will hurt someone's feelings or have a mean or hateful tone.

When one of us in the group did one of the above-mentioned items, someone was supposed to say "red light." This meant the current conversation would stop, no explanation necessary, and the subject would be changed. In addition to these five suggestions, I welcomed input from the entire family on how to improve communication for the betterment of everyone.

At our next family gathering a few weeks later, it appeared to me that not one person was attempting to practice any of the five suggestions. They either forgot all about them or, contrary to what they had led me to believe when I first asked for their help, my suggestions were really not something they wanted to try.

I was still depressed and angry and felt bad about myself for complaining, saying "I hate" on a regular basis and using words like "stupid" and "crazy." Being in no mood to point out the rules again, I felt like I was fighting a losing battle. Why should I have to remind my family members or ask them over and over again? Shouldn't they be so concerned about my state of mind that they would voluntarily want to help me and put forth their best effort? All I could do was practice these things on my own for my mental health and satisfaction. If others in the family weren't willing to try, then they probably did not recognize that they did these things or they didn't want to change.

After completing the four-hour anger management course with the female counselor, I realized the mad conversations in my head that I so desperately wanted to get rid of were still there. I asked myself why the anger management course had failed. I was angry that I was angry, which made me madder than I was before. I wanted the anger to go away that instant, and I was fed up with myself because I hadn't succeeded in ridding myself of it. At that moment, I realized that anger is like fire: If isn't treated, it rapidly spreads. The fire had to be put out or it would just continue to burn and smolder, charring everyone in its path.

Before attending counseling, I was just angry. Now I was angry *because* I was angry, and I hated that. It was a horrible feeling, and not knowing how to fix it was an equally horrible feeling.

So I signed up for a couples counseling session. This session consisted of my female counselor, her husband, my husband, and me. My husband was involved so he could contribute his thoughts and perspectives on the situation. Little did I know this couples session would turn into a huge debacle resulting in further thoughts of suicide and never seeing either counselor again.

Counseling Debacle

The male counselor began the session by asking my husband why he was attending couples therapy. My husband said he was there to support his wife, get to the bottom of the situation, and make whatever changes were necessary.

The man immediately took a liking to my husband. But as time went on, the male counselor was the only one who talked, and it was apparent he did not want me to speak up.

For two hours, this man berated and belittled me. When I tried to give my point of view, he immediately told me to be quiet, that he wasn't finished, and then he again told me about what my problems were and how he knew exactly what I needed to do to straighten up.

After going on and on about his horrific mother and abusive childhood, he accused me of living in a tiny box and needing to figure out *who* I was, not *what* I was. In addition, he lectured me on forgiveness, stated my problems were petty and unimportant, and told me to quit acting like I knew everything. Mentioning that his wife took immaculate notes, he said he knew exactly how I needed to be treated and talked to.

I was astounded by all this because not only had I never spoken to him as a counselor before but, prior to this, his wife never took notes during our sessions! She may have jotted down some notes after our session was over, but she never wrote down a word during any of our sessions.

I cried through the entire couples session. By the time the male counselor was done—the female counselor never said a word to defend me or support me, sitting there like she too was terrified to open her mouth at any time—I was at the bottom of the barrel. I finally yelled, "I don't deserve this! All I want to do is kill myself, and you're making things worse!"

I was angry with my husband for sitting there quietly, not saying a word to defend me and permitting the man to talk to me like that. I didn't know it at the time, but my husband was wondering what kind of bogus therapy I had been going to and later felt guilty for not pulling me out of there as soon as he realized things had turned sour.

The male counselor usually dealt with other men, usually individuals, who were mandated by the court system to take anger management classes. I realized that with some of the folks he dealt with, being tough and getting the upper hand might be the best way to go. But I had voluntarily enrolled in these classes. I had never been arrested nor had any trouble with the law. I was just trying to work out my stress, anxiety, and fears and thought anger management could help.

After the session, my husband drove home, as I was in no condition to do so. I laid around the rest of the evening, sulking, not wanting to eat, and trying to figure out how things had gone so terribly wrong when the past counseling sessions with the woman had all turned out well.

The next afternoon, my husband forced me to get out of the house and go to the movies. I protested, as all I wanted to do was crawl into a deep, dark hole and slowly melt away. I reluctantly went to the movie, although I have no memory of it. My deep depression and feelings of worthlessness and purposelessness were so overwhelming I couldn't focus on anything but being unfairly berated by the male counselor.

I was stumped because I had no idea how to forgive him for what he'd done; I was stuck in my own mind between a rock and hard place. I asked my husband, "How? Tell me how to do it, and I'll do it." My husband said, "No one can tell you how; you just have to do it yourself." I thought to myself, "Great. Thanks. What kind of help is that?"

Feeling foolish and unable to do the simplest thing requested of me, I realized that no matter what your goal is, you cannot look outside yourself for help. Inside is where you find all the answers. Inside is where you find courage, forgiveness, and determination. Whatever goal you seek—whether it is losing weight, writing a book, or being a "better you"—no one else can do it for you. You have to do it all yourself, whether you like it or not.

So now what was I supposed to do? Who do you turn to when counseling with the professionals doesn't work?

Class Rules

Have you ever cleaned out your filing cabinet and found something you forgot you had but was surprised and excited that you found it? Soon after looking for ways to improve my attitude and negative outlook on life, I found *Twenty Characteristics of Successful Women* and *Class Rules.* I do not remember from whom or where I obtained either of these, and I am unaware of the original authors, but each of these is witty and astute. I found them very helpful at the time I found them. I hope you will too even though you may not be in a class room setting or business executive as most of these items apply to everyday life. Enjoy.

Twenty Characteristics of Successful Women

1. Have a high degree of integrity
2. Demonstrate effective listening and communication skills
3. Honor own emotions
4. Are creative

5. Take charge of own life
6. Are caring and sensitive to others' needs
7. Give praise and recognition to self
8. Give praise and recognition to others
9. Solicit support for self
10. Delegate work effectively
11. Keep a positive outlook
12. Are open to change
13. Good at problem solving
14. Are flexible
15. Approach tasks/situations prepared—homework done
16. Communicate benefits, not limitations
17. Look at the big picture—global thinking
18. Understand timing
19. Are intuitive
20. Network, network, network!

Class Rules

- Have ideas that no one has ever had before. You can, you know.
- Whatever you are doing, never stop growing, developing, seeking, inquiring, sensing. Seize life with ferocity and maximize every moment.
- Encourage the growth and development of others. Stifling the growth of anyone (child, wife, parent, lover, neighbor, stranger, husband, student, teacher) is a crime against humanity. When any one person grows, we all grow.
- Grow in many directions. Learn to reason, play, work hard, and strive and learn to just sit and relax. Learn to love yourself and others. Keep your body, mind, and spirit in tip-top shape.
- Be sincere, not serious. Have fun. Enjoy yourself. It's easier than you think.

- Be responsible. Come to class. Come prepared to challenge and to be challenged. Task yourself, your peers, and your teacher.
- Read far into the night. Go to films, not movies. Handle CD's and DVD's with care.
- Work. If you work, it will lead to growth. Aim for quality.
- Travel. See the world. Meet as many people as you can. Make many friends. Have a few very, very close friends.
- There are no ultimate truths. Not even the previous statement is always true. Truth is a function of space and time.
- Don't try to reason and create at the same time. They're two different processes and, for goodness sake, don't program anything before it's created and reasoned.
- Keep a diary. Communicate with yourself. Write letters to your friends, former teachers, and elected representatives.
- Every once in a while, throw out all the rules and start over.
- When you think there is nothing left to learn or that you know it all, you've stopped growing. Seek help immediately. You may already be dead!

I posted *Class Rules, Twenty Characteristics of Successful Women*, and an anger management cheat sheet on the wall in my office, right by the light switch, so I could remind myself of these things. I read them every day, hoping to retrain my brain. These tools gave me hope and reassurance that I would find whatever it was I was looking for.

A Different Counselor Altogether

I knew I needed help soon or I would end all my suffering myself. Having had the couples session go so badly and knowing full well that I still needed therapy, I went online and found another counselor in the Dallas/Fort Worth area, a certified depression and anger management counselor who also treated individuals and couples with pregnancy and relationship issues, sexual-identity exploration, and eating disorders. She had more than ten years' professional counseling experience.

At our first session, she sat down, kicked off her shoes, and asked how she could help me. I liked her immediately. She was soft spoken and laid back and had a completely different attitude than the previous female counselor.

Every month for the next two years, I made an appointment with her until we finally resolved my anger issue. By this time, my physical illnesses had all disappeared, and I could focus on getting back on my feet mentally and emotionally.

Gratitude Journal

During my first visit, my counselor suggested I start a gratitude journal. I'd heard of others using them before but never thought I needed to sit down and write about what I was thankful for. But I was wrong again.

Every night before turning in, I would write down three things I was grateful for. I wrote down anything, even if I thought it was trivial. Soon I had a list of everything good in my life, from family and friends and being in good health to driving a nice car and not being in debt. Gratitude is endless if you're willing to acknowledge it, and you'd be surprised at all the things you take for granted on a daily basis. Things like your eyesight, being able to walk and get around, and even running water, an indoor toilet, and electricity—in the old days, no one had any of these things.

I kept my journal for about a month. After that, I included all the things I was grateful for in my nightly prayers.

In the beginning, a gratitude journal might seem ridiculous, but in the end, you'll be thankful for everything you have, including the roof over your head and the warm bed you sleep in. Being thankful for the small things puts life in perspective. You'll remember that you started out with nothing and worked hard for everything that you have. You'll realize you were born with absolutely nothing and that you nor anyone else is entitled to anything.

Even though you will meet others who have more than you and may seem to "have it all," you'll still be thankful for what you have. If you live your life wishing you had more—more money, fame, clothes, children, and so on—you'll end up hating your life because you concentrate on what you don't have. A gratitude journal will force you to focus on what you *do* have. And trust me, you have a lot, even if it doesn't seem like it at the present moment.

Have you ever felt sorry for an elderly person you see sitting on the porch of a run-down house with no paint, broken windows, and weeds growing out of control? I catch myself doing it quiet often. But how do you know that elderly person isn't happy with the beat-up old house and tall weeds? Maybe the person is out of work or lives off a small disability or Social Security check every month. That person is happy to have a roof over his or her head and not have dozens of bills to pay. And maybe there are tall weeds, but the person isn't in debt from buying a lawn mower or paying a gardener. And despite being out of work, he or she still has food in the pantry and a heater to keep him or her warm on a cold winter's day.

Maybe the person has no expectations of being rich, famous, or better off than the neighbors. This person is happy with what little he or she has because it's more than what he or she had ten or twenty years before. The key to happiness is wanting what you have, not having what you want.

Personality Test

Often, my new therapist gave me homework, an assignment I had to complete before coming back for the next appointment.

During my second visit, she asked me to go home and take a brief online personality test. Having never taken one before, I had no idea what to expect and was kind of interested and amused at the idea.

After logging on to www.similarminds.com, I spent the next fifteen minutes taking what they claim to be the "most detailed personality assessment on the Internet." With a little over 100 questions, ranging from true/false and multiple choice to a rating system that involved answering with "sometimes," "never," "always," etc., the test was interesting and easy to complete.

At the end, the results popped up in a few seconds. My results on February 10, 2009, were as follows (the higher the percentage, the more dominant the trait):

Type 1. Perfectionism	78%
Type 2. Helpfulness	47%
Type 3. Image Focus	30%
Type 4. Hypersensitivity	57%
Type 5. Detachment	42%
Type 6. Anxiety	54%
Type 7. Adventurousness	27%
Type 8. Aggressiveness	37%
Type 9. Calmness	31%

(My husband took the test as well, just for fun. His highest scores were on helpfulness, anxiety, and calmness as the highest at 64%. His lowest were hypersensitivity at 35% and adventurousness at 40%).

At the time, I really had no clue I was a perfectionist, and I had always thought of perfectionism as being good, not bad. Over the course of my therapy, I realized more and more that I really did not want to be a perfectionist, that perfectionism is a huge dysfunction.

According to the University of Illinois Counseling Center (www.counselingcenter.illinois.edu/) perfectionism refers to a set of self-defeating thoughts and behaviors aimed at reaching excessively high unrealistic goals. Perfectionism taken to extremes as paraphrased from Wikipedia is considered to be unhealthful because it can result in anxiety and low self-esteem and put individuals at risk of OCD, eating disorders, being a workaholic, self-harm, and clinical depression. A perfectionist's greatest fear is to be flawed.

Perfectionists are people who are always the most critical of others. You know the types, the ones who point out what you've done wrong and never praise you for all the things you've done right. They point out the one misspelled word in your three hundred-word blog entry or e-mail communication. They're the ones who complain that the bed still has wrinkles it in after it's been made, that you didn't close the blinds after leaving the house, that you didn't bring in the mail for the day.

I no longer wanted to be a perfectionist—or hypersensitive either, for that matter. Complaining, ridiculing others, and being an inflexible perfectionist only makes you unhappy and causes discord with others in your life, including friends, relatives, and the people you meet every day.

Children raised by perfectionist parents feel unloved, guilty, worthless, and rejected when they make a mistake. As adults, these children will be filled with self-blame and self-criticism instead of self-forgiveness, even for events that are not their fault. It happened to me. I hated and blamed myself for possibly being a diabetic, the death of my guinea pig, and totaling my van. At the time, those things were unforgivable in my mind.

The Wonderful Wisdom of Wayne Dyer

In February 2009, about the time I found the new therapist and was searching for a "better me," I discovered two CDs that changed my attitude and poor outlook on life: *Everyday Wisdom* and *101 Ways to Transform Your Life* by Dr. Wayne W. Dyer.

I'd lie in bed before going to sleep every night and listen to these CDs over and over again until I could practically recite them. Dr. Dyer's deep, calm, soothing voice is perfect right before bedtime. (I'm sure he'll be thrilled to learn he goes to bed with me every night.)

This nightly ritual now takes the place of watching the news, which I find to be predominantly negative and violent. I go to sleep relaxed, having reinforced positive, kind thoughts for the next day.

Below, I've listed my twenty favorite beneficial transformational thoughts from Dr. Dyer. It was not easy to narrow down two wonderful CDs to just twenty thoughts, but I chose the ones that have had the most impact on my negative attitudes and the ones I have made a conscious attempt at instituting in my "new" life. I repeat these thoughts to myself day after day to keep them in my mind at all times. Eventually, a little at a time, you will believe them and start practicing them in real life. I hope they will help you as much as they did me.

My Twenty Favorite Transformational Thoughts From Dr. Dyer

1. Tame your ego.
2. You are what you think about.
3. Be a hostage to your ego or a host to God.
4. Progress is impossible if you do things the way you've always done them.
5. If you have a choice between being right and being kind, always choose to be kind.
6. The difference between success and failure is perception.
7. You are not a human having a spiritual experience but a spirit having a human experience.
8. Have a mind that is open to everything and attached to nothing.
9. There are no justified resentments.
10. Be better than you used to be.
11. Be independent despite the good opinion of others.
12. Love everyone unconditionally.
13. You are born with all the knowledge and wisdom you need to know; it is all inside you.

14. Nothing is good or bad; everything is neutral.
15. In my world, nothing ever goes wrong; it is all as it should be.
16. You do not attract what you want; you attract what you are.
17. You can't solve problems with the same mind that created them.
18. You are not your reputation; you are not what you do, and you are not what you have.
19. Do everything when you know it is from the heart and detach from the outcome.
20. Forgive yourself for your transgressions. See that mistakes are lessons for you to transcend.(To purchase any of Dr. Dyer's forty-plus wonderful books and CDs, go to www.drwaynedyer.com or www.hayhouse.com.)

I took the thoughts and affirmations from Dr. Dyer as well as Louise Hay, and Sylvia Browne that I really believed in and felt could improve my attitude and outlook on life and wrote them out on a piece of paper. I kept writing until I had more than six sheets of these affirmations written down. Then I posted laminated notecards with the sayings on them and taped them around my house. Anywhere I went, I would see them and stop to read them. I put notecards in the kitchen, on the bathroom mirror, and on walls and closet doors. Three affirmations adorn the mirror in my bathroom even today:

1. Today is entirely up to me.
2. I can do anything in Christ who gives me strength.
3. In my world, nothing ever goes wrong; everything is as it should be.

It's now official: I've become exactly like my old roommate, the one I used think was a total dork for sticking self-help affirmations on the walls. As someone who today owns more than twenty Wayne Dyer CDs and listens to them on a regular basis, I shudder at my old opinion of my former roommate. I now realize he was a happy, well-balanced, extremely smart man. Early in life, he managed to succeed in something that still eluded me twenty years later: finding happiness and being grateful and satisfied with what you have. He wasn't a robot or an alien from outer space after all, but he did possess a secret—the secret of self-help, self-improvement, and living in a state of gratitude every day of his life.

Meditation

Soon after discovering Dr. Wayne Dyer and Sylvia Browne, I took up meditation. Sitting in a comfortable chair with all the lights off, I would close my eyes, say my prayers and affirmations, and meditate for about twenty minutes. Sometimes I would sit on the swing out on the patio and just listen to the whistling birds, the chirping bugs, and the howling dogs. Every now and then, I'd open my eyes to see a few deer wandering around the front yard.

At first, I wondered if I was meditating correctly. But there really is no wrong way to meditate. My main goal was to relax and let go of my daily stress. Clearing my mind as best I could, I just sat and listened, not thinking of what I needed to do the next day or what went on throughout that day; I was just "sittin' on the dock of the bay," so to speak, watching the world pass by and not worrying about what the future would bring. Just living in the moment was refreshing and quite a new experience for me.

When you live with chronic anger, living in the moment is almost impossible because your thoughts are too busy ruminating over past events or worrying about what might happen in the days to come. I realized I have no control over tomorrow and cannot change the past. The present moment is where all the power is, where happiness is, and where we all must live our lives in order to make the most of them.

Meditating has many benefits, and it is something that can be done anywhere at any time. People don't have to meditate every single time with their legs crossed and their hands open on their knees. Sometimes I meditate in the car for a minute while I'm stopped at a traffic light. I don't close my eyes; I just breathe deeply and think of very little. Or maybe I'll do a short meditation during a commercial while watching television or while lying in bed as I doze off. Depending on how often and what benefits you derive from this practice, you can meditate several times a day without anyone ever knowing what you're doing.

Emotional Freedom Technique

Early in my therapy, a friend referred me to a woman in Dallas who specializes in the Emotional Freedom Technique, or EFT. This woman's house was very quiet, quaint, and nicely decorated.

I briefly explained my past medical conditions, accidents, and attitudes and then we started Energy Tapping or Energy Meridian Therapy, other names for EFT. This technique is a process discovered by the Chinese more than five thousand years ago and involves tapping on one of more of the ten meridian points on the body. While tapping, a person repeats the following statement three times: "Even though I [whatever issue you are working on], I deeply and completely love and accept myself." The human body's meridian points are the eyebrow, the side of the eye, under the eye, under the nose, the chin crease, the collarbone, under the arm, the top of the head, the thymus gland (located in the middle of the chest below breast bone), and the karate chop (located on the side of the hand below the pinky finger).

So for several minutes at a time, I sat on this woman's sofa, tapping various parts of my body, repeating the statement for everything that was bothering me. "Even though I am angry, overweight, eat poorly, always tired, afraid of getting an illness, not getting along with family and friends, I deeply and completely love and accept myself."

I took tapping instructions and a list of energy meridians home with me so I could practice on my own at my own pace. I tried the tapping a few times in the shower for fear of looking like a fool in front of my husband (who didn't outright say he thought it was all hogwash, but I suspected he did). I found myself thinking I was like a monkey or something, talking to myself in the shower and tapping on my head and then my eyes, chin, chest, and side. If you have ever thought you looked (or felt) ridiculous doing a task, activity, or sport, like trying to rub your tummy and pat your head at the same time, the EFT might make you feel totally and completely foolish the first few times you do it. It did me anyway. Maybe if I had had someone to participate with me, I wouldn't have felt so foolish, but going in the shower privately and secretly so one would know kind of made me feel ashamed and embarrassed or like I was doing something wrong. I did it a few times and then just let it slip away.

Many people have great EFT success stories; others don't. Maybe it would have made me feel better and less angry or maybe not. But I still chalked it up to another failure in my quest for defeating anger.

Maybe I was expecting a miracle, an overnight cure. As someone who has never had a lot of patience, I tend to expect immediate results and perfection the first time I try something, no matter what it is that I am doing, even today. Back then, if I didn't see immediate results, I gave up and considered myself a failure.

Church

My new counselor also encouraged me to go to church so I could meet new people and make new friends who held the same beliefs about God that I did. The churches I liked the best were the Unitarian Universalist and the Unity churches. The people weren't forceful in trying to convert others, and the services didn't involve people rambling about how everyone is a sinner and we all go to hell. I even found one church with huge glass windows so parishioners could look out during the service and watch the trees blowing in the gentle breeze and the squirrels playing in the rain with streaks of sunlight shining through the branches.

I tend to get "the creeps" when I walk into a church with no windows and, right in front of the pews, the only thing to look at is a huge painting that looks like stained glass, with Jesus Christ hanging on the cross with blood dripping from his hands and feet. When I see that, I just turn around and leave. I've always thought church should be a happy, peaceful place, and I can't think of anything less peaceful than a constant reminder of a bleeding, dead Jesus nailed to a cross.

While at a Unitarian Universalist church, I met some folks who were talking about a religious and spiritual belief quiz they took on the Internet. A married couple said the quiz matched up their beliefs with that of a liberal Quaker. I was stunned. "A what? You mean Quaker, like the guy on the oatmeal box? That's a religion?"

My curiosity got the better of me, so I rushed home and quickly logged on to www.beliefnet.com. The "Belief-O-Matic" quiz is a set of twenty short and relatively simple questions about whether you believe in one god or multiple gods, reincarnation, life after death, or the devil and what you believe about the purpose and causes of suffering in the world. At the end, it ranks a list of twenty-six religions your beliefs most closely align with. I most closely aligned with a liberal Quaker and was second most closely aligned with Unitarian Universalism; the last three religions I aligned with were Roman Catholic, Jehovah's Witness, and the Church of Jesus Christ of Latter-Day Saints.

Days later, my entire family and a few friends said they were curious about what religious belief they aligned with. We took turns using the computer, taking the test, and laughing hysterically over the odd results that none of us expected. My husband aligned with the Baha'i faith; my mother aligned with Orthodox Quaker; and our two Mormon friends were most closely aligned with—you guessed it—the Church of Jesus Christ of

Latter-Day Saints. (I was dying to know if their tests would tell them they were some other religion or indeed Mormon.)

Dream Interpretation

I've suffered from nightmares my entire life. Not just bad dreams but dreams about doing something wrong, being a screwup, and not measuring up to others' expectations. After my counselor suggested I was suffering from anxiety dreaming, I got curious and did a little research on my own.

For a few months, I studied dreams and how to interpret them, hoping my dreams would turn into pleasant, happy ones instead of those filled with pain and misery.

While studying my dreams, wanting to rid myself of horrible, self-defeating nightmares, I found several good resources. Carl Jung has a great CD called *Interpretation of Dreams* that I listen to over and over again. I also purchased the books *Dreams: Close Your Eyes, Open Your Mind* by Tucker Shaw and *10,000 Dreams Interpreted* by Gustavus Hindman Miller.

I began my journaling by answering these seven questions from Shaw's book:

1. What is the mood of your dream?
2. What is the setting of your dream?
3. Who are the characters in your dream?
4. What things are in your dream?
5. What is the plot of your dream?
6. How does your dream end?
7. What's the title of your dream?

My dreams did improve for a while, but after a few months, they reverted back to horror. Even today, I still suffer from nightmares almost every night. While studying my dreams, I kept a journal, writing down everything I could remember about my nightmares. Here's a sample of my entries:

- I dreamt that hair was growing in my mouth. I'd try to pull it out, but it just kept growing longer and faster. I'd hurry to pull it all out and shut my mouth, thinking it wouldn't grow with my mouth shut, but it did. I pulled and pulled and pulled, but it all grew back just as fast as I pulled it out.

- One of my recurring dreams is that I am going through college but missing all my classes because I am too busy being The Creature Teacher. These two events did not occur at the same time in my life, so it baffles me as to why they occur together in my dreams. I would go to class sporadically, feel totally lost, get frustrated over not being able to complete my classes, and eventually drop out. I'd tell myself I don't need a degree, as I already have a great job making good money and the degree won't necessarily mean a pay raise. Year after year, I try to go to college but never graduate. I find this dream very odd, as I graduated college in 1988, after three intense years of study, with a bachelor of science degree in animal science.
- Another recurring dream is that I leave all my animals in the car on a hot sunny day and return to find them dead. This dream is horrible, as it directly relates to my current career. However, never in fifteen years of business have I ever left my car parked in the sunshine with no air conditioning, killing an animal.
- When I graduated from high school, I sold my horse so I could have ample time for my studies and obtain a degree. But today, in my forties, I still dream that I've boarded my horse at a stable but have forgotten where. I go for months without ever thinking of the poor critter and then one day realize I haven't fed, ridden, or cared for him in months. I drive around looking for the stable, but either it isn't where I thought it was or I just can't remember how to get there. The times that I manage to find the stable, I can't find my horse. I run around asking other people where my horse is, but they don't know who I am or have any idea of which horse is mine.

Dream interpretation is difficult and complex. *10,000 Dreams Interpreted* gives explanations about what it means to dream about animals, people, bathrooms or being on the toilet, storms, arguing, eating, food, etc. But interpretation depends not only on what you dream about but also on the context of the dream. One person dreaming about being chased could have a whole different meaning from someone else's "chase" dream. By the way, the top five nightmares most people experience, according to Shaw, are these:

1. Falling
2. Being chased by wild animals or monsters
3. Being naked in front of other people
4. Fire or natural disaster
5. Teeth falling out

I've experienced all these dream scenarios more than once. And believe it or not, many of these dreams were due to anxiety, fear of losing control of something in your current life, feeling uprepared, or being angry with someone or someone being angry with you.

Amazingly, most of us tend to remember our nightmares in more detail and more often than our happy, pleasant dreams. Analyzing my dreams was sort of fun; it shed a little light on my current feelings and thoughts. But unfortunately, it didn't get rid of my nightmares. I've become used to the idea that I will have nightmares until the day I die. Even with the help of Prozac since my dysthymia diagnosis, I am still haunted by nightmares every night and have no idea how to shake them.

Anxiety and More Anxiety

In May 2010, I purchased *The Anxiety and Phobia Workbook* by Dr. Edmund J. Bourne. I purchased this book after a woman hired me to bring my snakes to her house and meet with her therapist in an attempt to relieve her phobia of snakes. She hated snakes with a passion and trembled and cried when she saw them. I stayed at her house for an hour and half, and by the time I left, she was touching and holding my snakes. She said she didn't love them, but she understood them a little better and knew what to do if she encountered one in her yard.

When I conveyed to my therapist the joy and excitement I had experienced in helping this woman, she encouraged me to develop this service to help other people with a phobia of snakes, spiders, bugs, etc. While shopping at the bookstore, I thought *The Anxiety and Phobia Workbook* would help me understand specific phobias a little better and gain some insight into helping others with phobias.

The Anxiety and Phobia Workbook provides self-diagnosis questionnaires to help you identify what specific disorder or phobia you might you have.

While reading the book, I realized it wasn't really going to be helpful in dealing with animal-phobic clients, but it sure was helpful in assessing my own disorder and mental anguish.

Anxiety, according to *Merriam-Webster*, is a state of being uneasy, apprehensive, or worried about what may happen, having concern about a possible future event.

I had never really felt phobic about going outside, being around people, being in enclosed spaces, being exposed to germs, etc., but I did believe I could have some kind of anxiety disorder or a mild OCD. According to Wikipedia, OCD is the fourth most common mental disorder and is diagnosed nearly as often as asthma and diabetes.

About thirteen pages into the book was a section on GAD, or generalized anxiety disorder. GAD is often seen with depression disorders and can develop at any age. It affects women more than men and is seen in approximately 4 percent of the American population. Symptoms include:

- Restlessness or feeling keyed up
- Irritability
- Muscle tension
- Sleep difficulties
- Concentration difficulties
- Being easily tired or fatigued

Oh my, I experienced all these symptoms on a regular basis. In fact, my restlessness and irritability were about to come to a dramatic climax.

Intrigued, I read a little further to the section on OCD, suspecting I might have a mild case of that as well, with more obsessive tendencies than compulsive ones. I wasn't surprised to read that 2 to 3 percent of the general population may suffer from OCD in varying degrees, and that 25 percent of those with OCD are afflicted only with obsessions that may be based on fears of inflicting harm on a loved one.

The Anxiety and Phobia Handbook gives two questions to answer about OCD:

1. Do you have recurring intrusive thoughts such as hurting or harming a close relative, being contaminated with dirt or a

toxic substance, fearing you forgot to lock your door or turn off an appliance, or an unpleasant fantasy of catastrophe? (You recognize these thoughts as irrational, but you can't keep them from coming into your mind.)

2. Do you perform ritualistic actions such as washing your hands, checking, or counting to relieve anxiety over irrational fears that enter your mind?

Well, I often feared that I didn't lock the doors and that my house would burn down while I was not home. I also had fears of being raped or beaten or drowning after driving off a bridge. I count, on occasion, such as when I use stairs, and have a horrible habit of picking the skin off my cuticles and fingers, sometimes until they bleed and become so raw that I have to bandage them. I pick my skin when I'm bored, anxious, or just restless. I hate myself for picking and hurting myself. I have tried to stop on my own many times but never with any lasting success. (Although I was never clinically diagnosed with OCD or GAD, all these symptoms, including the skin picking and the invasive thoughts of fear, diminished or went away completely once I started taking Prozac.)

While reading *Awakened Instincts* by psychic MaryRose Occhino, I wrote down a list of fears—my deepest, darkest, most terrifying fears:

- Being useless, inferior to others, or helpless
- Not getting to do all the things in life that I want to do
- Losing my job and not having enough money to pay my bills
- Being diagnosed with a chronic disease or illness or sustaining an injury
- Being embarrassed or humiliated in public or by friends or coworkers
- Being disliked or knowing people hate me
- Being yelled at or arguing with someone and not knowing what to say or how to defend myself
- Being sued or robbed
- Being in a car accident

I realized I had lived a majority of my life making decisions based on fear. If many fears take over your life, you live a sheltered existence, taking few risks and seldom trying new and exciting things. I hated being fearful of just about everything, and I hated worrying about what others thought of me or the things I do or try.

Botched Vacation

By the summer of 2010, I was still trying to stifle the angry thoughts and feelings. I was ready to leave my husband, quit my job, and move to another country. I wanted a whole new life. I wanted to be someone else. It didn't matter who—just anyone other than who I was. I hated being me. Anybody else's life would have been better than mine. I wanted to be like Julia Roberts in *Eat, Pray, Love* and just drop everything and move away to a strange land with new environments, people, and foods. I felt stale, burned out, and old and just couldn't stand my life.

To further complicate matters, I felt guilty for having those feelings. I had a great life. My husband was kind and considerate and had a great sense of humor. My job was the best—I played with animals and kids all day long—what could be better than that? I lived in a beautiful home out in the country and had many "extras" like a boat and a Jet Ski watercraft. My bills were paid, I wasn't in debt, and I was finally healthy again. And yet I was miserable and couldn't figure out why or how to rid myself of these negative thoughts and feelings.

Was I having a midlife crisis? I'd always heard about them but never really knew anyone who'd had one and wondered if they were real. Could it be that, at forty-four years old, I just wanted a change, something different or more challenging?

In August 2010, my husband and I took off to Missouri for a weeklong vacation to celebrate our twelfth anniversary. But the celebration lasted only three days before we packed up and headed home. We had gotten into a small spat on the drive to Missouri; I got mad and stayed mad, as usual. (See Chapter 8, "No Coincidences," for details about our spat.) I told him I wanted a divorce—no negotiation or counseling, I just wanted out. The trip back home was uncomfortably silent.

To my surprise, I didn't qualify for a loan to purchase my own house, and with both our incomes pooled together, my husband and I barely qualified for a home in a low-income neighborhood. Renting was not an option, as no sane landlord would rent a dwelling to someone with more than forty pets. My husband and I both made good money, but the economy had hit a recession a few years prior, and the real estate market was suffering in a big way.

In 2001, when we first moved to Texas, my husband and I easily qualified for the same loan we were struggling to get in 2010. The real estate industry had tightened down on who they gave loans to and, to our surprise, we qualified for only half of what we planned on.

As a mental health professional, my counselor could not and would not condone divorce. After an entire session over the phone, she convinced me to give couples counseling another try with another counselor she recommended. Our appointment was two weeks later.

I Want Out!

The last few months before I was diagnosed with dysthymia were a whirlwind of emotions. I woke up angry, went to bed angry, and was angry every minute of every day. Even when I had perfectly good days, where nothing went wrong, I was still mad. I didn't want to live that way anymore.

I felt the most peace and contentment when I was working. I loved being around kids and animals, and my job allowed me to do both at the same time. The fun, enjoyment, and pleasure of being a wildlife educator far outweighed the few negative aspects of the profession.

Educating children, whether it was one child or three hundred children at a time, gave me joy and relief from the other tumultuous uprisings that were stirring in my personal life. During each presentation, I became totally immersed in the here and now, the immediate moment and what I was there to accomplish. I was not thinking or obsessing over all the things and people that had infuriated me up until that moment. My time working was the only time I really felt "in the moment." Believe or not, many of my clients have actually complimented me on my patience and communication skills with children.

More often than not, my anger was directed toward and inflamed by those unexpected, unwanted events and circumstances that made decision making, rationalizing, and using common sense painstakingly difficult and filled me with self-doubt and worry about not meeting others' expectations—or even my own, for that matter.

After I was done working for the day, I'd always feel the anger creeping up on me during the drive home. Uncontrollable emotions regarding past events always came to the surface, and my unhappiness took over until the next birthday party, school assembly, or Scout show where I could focus 100 percent on the task at hand, not thinking or worrying about simple annoyances and mishaps that had otherwise consumed my every thought.

Every few months, it seemed I was on an emotional roller coaster: happy for a few days and then less happy and then continuing downhill until I spent a few days extremely depressed and hopeless. I would climb up only to fall down into a ditch again, feeling stuck and hopeless and not knowing how to pick myself back up and move on. Why couldn't I control my feelings and emotions?

During the past few months, I had made meditation a regular habit, said my prayers and affirmations daily, and practiced deep breathing. Every day, over and over again, I performed positive mental and emotional techniques with only temporary relief. For a few days, I'd feel great and then one day I would wake up feeling like overnight, I'd forgotten everything I'd learned. All the new methods of coping were not working. It seemed as though I just woke up one morning feeling mad for no reason. I begged my therapist to help me.

One day, my husband found me in bed, crying hysterically. I told him I just wanted out. He asked, "Out of what?" But I couldn't say. I had nothing concrete or specific to give him. I just screamed, "I want out! I need to be somewhere or do something, but I don't know where I'm supposed to be or what I'm supposed to do."

All I knew was that I felt lost and like I was living another person's life. I wasn't where I was supposed to be. I just wanted out. I felt trapped inside my own head—claustrophobic, like my thoughts were banging up against my skull, trying to get out. It was excruciatingly painful, miserable, and terrifying all at the same time.

I didn't understand at the time, but I certainly do now: I wanted out of *my head*. I wanted out of the anger and obsessive conversations in my head, yelling and screaming at others who weren't even present at the time. I wanted out of the anger and madness that had taken over my mind, my relationships, my life. I just wanted it all to stop so I could be normal like everybody else.

My husband asked me to hang in there, as we had an appointment with the new couples therapist in less than a week. He held me and we laid there on the bed while I cried until I couldn't cry anymore. I hoped and longed for our next session with the new counselor to help me find the answer and give some meaning and peace to my life.

Our second couples counselor was very nice and intelligent and seemed genuinely concerned about our situation. But the second session ended in disaster. My husband and I both left the counselor's office in tears, confident our marriage was over. My husband begged me not to leave but offered his support with the move.

A Slave to Anger

For the first time in my life and my marriage, I wished I had married someone my own age and started a family. This thought was terrifying and daunting to my soul, as I loved my husband with all my heart. But at the same time, I couldn't help obsessing over what my life would be like when he was gone.

My husband has three grown children, two of whom are older than me, so I'd never been considered a stepmom by myself or his children. Always too afraid of screwing up as a parent, I never wanted children of my own when I was in my twenties. Now in my forties, married to a man in his seventies, reality hit me like a giant weight: If my husband passed away first, I'd have to remarry or be completely alone in my "golden years." Again, the guilt took over and more depression set in.

I felt unloved, unappreciated, and taken advantage of, like I didn't matter to anyone else, including my husband or my immediate family. I'd suffered the consequences of losing a friend and a sister and felt the few people still in my life didn't care about what I was going through or understand the severity of my aching soul.

My mother never called to ask if I was OK, angry, or upset or to ask what specifically was making life difficult for me. In fact, if she wanted to know something about me, she'd phone my husband while I was at work to "check on me."

I'd always been a mama's girl, and my sister was always our daddy's little girl. My mother and I phoned each other several times a week throughout my young adulthood, but when I started therapy, I felt the need to cut the apron strings. My mother is a complainer; nothing and no one in this world will ever meet her standards, and she doesn't realize that her standards are hers, not everyone else's.

People all over the world live their lives according to their own standards, not what others expect of them. When my mother complains, I walk away, either out of the house altogether or to another room, becoming absorbed in another activity. For me to grow, ditch my negativity, and end my vicious cycle of ranting and raving, the last thing I needed or wanted to hear was complaining, and the last thing I wanted to do was get sucked into someone else's problems. I needed to grow up, be my own person, solve my own problems, and not run to others every time something threw me for a loop. I felt bad about being a burden to others, always asking for advice and feeling completely stuck over small matters and decisions.

After crying on the phone to my therapist time and time again, hopeless and frustrated, I asked her why no one in her field had found the cause of chronic anger. Why hadn't one psychologist been able to figure out what was causing the daily, unyielding anger that was sapping my soul of joy, happiness, and peace of mind? What causes some people to open their eyes in the morning, look around, and find themselves angry, irritated, and mad when they haven't even stepped out of bed yet? Why hadn't anyone discovered why anger management doesn't work on someone who has raging, mad thoughts day in and day out, even on a perfectly pleasant day?

I hated myself for being this way. Individuals who cannot master their anger become a slave to it. Anger had controlled every aspect of my life and psyche, from work and relationships to the important and trivial decisions I was forced to make every day. I was a slave, a servant doing what my anger ordered me to do. I wished I was "normal" like everyone else.

Affirmations only worked for me when I was "up"; they failed when I was "down." Frustrated at being up and down and up and down, I was steps away from just giving up altogether, convinced that nothing was going to work. I despised myself for not being able to change. The worst part was that after a few days of feeling good, being upbeat and anger free, I actually missed being mad—or it at least that's what it felt like. I was so accustomed to and comfortable with being angry every minute of every day, the feeling of happiness and contentment was strange and uncomfortable; I felt like I needed and desired to be angry. It almost felt better to be mad than to be happy.

I knew I couldn't live my entire life this way. I had to change or I would kill myself just to find relief from constant anger. I begged my therapist to help me. Crying over the phone, I pleaded with my counselor: "I will try anything. Tell me what to do and I'll do it. Can I try electroshock therapy, acupuncture, or an exorcism? What about pot brownies or hypnosis or a lobotomy? Anything. Just please get rid of my anger. Tell me what to do and I'll do it."

By this time, my counselor was more than baffled. On more than one occasion during my two years of therapy, she mentioned that I was the most self-motivated, persistent, and determined client she had ever met. Still unable to pinpoint the source of my anger and inability to control angry emotions and thoughts and witnessing my despair and longing for help of any kind, my therapist kindly recommended I go to a therapist for a mental evaluation.

On October 5, 2010, God sent down hope, happiness, and a solution to my turmoil and unrest.

Chapter 6

Bad State of Mind

An hour and half after the session began, the psychiatrist had been brought up to speed on my life, the counseling debacles, my illnesses, and my reactions to each one. We were almost finished—but not quite.

The Assessment

After being asked numerous questions about my thoughts, feelings, and behaviors, I was then asked to perform simple subtraction, counting back from one hundred to zero by increments of seven.

Math had never been my strong suit. What happened if I missed an answer by one? Or by five? What if I couldn't do it? Slowly, I started subtracting, being very careful before giving a final answer. The doctor stopped me when I hit fifty-one, convinced of my ability to complete the task.

I was then asked to memorize four random words, which I remember to this day: boat, tree, house, and rose. About ten minutes later, after more questions, I was asked to repeat the words back to him, which I did successfully without hesitation.

More questions followed, ranging from "Do you hear voices?" and "Do you think someone is following you?" to "How would you rate your anger on a scale of one to ten?" and "How often do you cry?" and "What makes you laugh or gives you pleasure?" and "Have you ever spent all day in bed, unable or not wanting to get up?"

I Have What?

Finally, the questions were over and a diagnosis of dysthymia was officially on the record. The psychiatrist wrote a prescription for an antidepressant, and we scheduled a follow-up appointment for four weeks later.

I felt relieved as I walked out of the office. Now, maybe my life could be normal; I could be like other people. Maybe the angry conversations in my head would subside, and I could live in the moment, not spending so much time dwelling on the past and all the people who had made me mad. Now, maybe all those affirmations and life-transforming thoughts could grab hold of me and have a permanent place in my spirit and psyche.

Not being familiar with this disorder or knowing anyone afflicted with it, I craved more information. I immediately went to the Internet when I arrived home. According to Wikipedia, dysthymia is "a mood disorder consisting of chronic depression but with less severity than major depressive disorder." Chronic, according to *Webster's New World College Dictionary*, means lasting a long time or recurring often; continuing indefinitely; perpetual and constant.

So there it was, the answer to my anger, frustration, and constant anxiety. For forty-four years I'd been suffering from depression that doesn't go away and can be the root of other negative emotions like excessive anger, anxiety, and frustration.

Dysthymia Facts

According to *Harvard Health Publications*, dysthymia is a Greek word that means "bad state of mind" or "ill humor." During my research on this "bad state of mind", I uncovered many interesting facts, including the following:

1. At least three-quarters of people with dysthymia also suffer from another psychiatric disorder, such as anxiety disorder, drug addiction, or alcoholism.
2. Dysthymia affects approximately 3 to 6 percent of the population and is associated with significant functional impairment.
3. Dysthymia is genetic and is two to three times more common in women than in men.
4. Individuals with dysthymia have a higher-than-average chance of developing major depression.

5. Dysthymia sufferers are often seen as "moody persons." They are often overly critical, constantly complaining and incapable of having fun.
6. Dysthymia often begins in childhood, adolescence, or early adulthood, but most people wait approximately ten years before seeking treatment. In children, this disorder is often associated with ADHD, conduct disorder, anxiety disorders, learning disorders, and mental retardation.
7. Dysthymic disorder happens in about 25 to 50 percent of people who have sleep abnormalities that cause a reduction in rapid eye movement sleep and also impaired sleep continuity.
8. Causes of dysthymia are complex and not yet completely understood. They range from sleep abnormalities, hormones, neurotransmitters, and upbringing to heredity and stress.
9. Dysthymia is common in the elderly, particularly after the death of a spouse or the onset of illness, including diabetes, Parkinson's disease, cancer, and heart disease.
10. More than 40 percent of women do not ask for professional help for treating dysthymia due to embarrassment. More than 50 percent of men and women do not seek help due to a belief that depression is a sign of weakness.
11. Among people with a form of depression, 80 percent will not seek help at all, and 90 percent of African American men suffering from depression will never receive help.
12. Dysthymia suffers are usually very capable of functioning in day-to-day life, like going to work, running errands, and doing everyday chores. However, they are more comfortable with particular routines that provide structure, stability, and certainty, especially if the individual also has some form of OCD, even a mild form.

Symptoms of Dysthymia

Symptoms of dysthymia are:

- Feelings of emptiness, hopelessness, or worthlessness
- Insomnia or hypersomnia

- Poor concentration or difficulty making decisions
- Low energy or fatigue
- Low self-esteem
- Low sex drive
- Social withdrawal
- Thoughts of death or suicide
- Poor appetite or overeating
- Excessive crying
- Irritability
- Chronic anxiety or worrying
- Excessive or inappropriate feeling of guilt
- Unable to remember when the last time he or she was happy, confident, or inspired

These symptoms tend to be less severe than major depression, but they do fluctuate in intensity. To be diagnosed, according to www.depressedtest.com/dysthymia.html, an adult must have two or more of these symptoms for at least two years.

I looked back on my life and thought about all the symptoms of dysthymia, how many of them I had, and how they related to the choices I'd made. I took out a piece of paper and began writing down what I perceived to be signs of my newfound mental disorder. This is what I wrote:

- Getting angry over little things that most people just get slightly irritated about
- Swearing and calling other people names
- A sense of entitlement, that I deserved what everyone else had and I resented those who were more successful and had more than me
- Thinking that little problems could not be solved
- Making a big deal out of a small incident
- Good mood one day and sad, mad, or depressed the next day
- Letting one negative event ruin my whole day
- Staying mad for days on end, without any relief

- Not speaking to those with whom I was mad
- Irritability over trivial matters
- Lack of sleep—sleeping well until 2 a.m. and then being awake for a few hours hours, only to fall back asleep around 6 a.m.
- Difficulty making decisions or seeing what my options were
- Low self-esteem—repeating to myself that I was fat, stupid, old, and ugly
- Sadness every month or so for no apparent reason, just feeling blah, not wanting to do anything
- Being close minded. No interest in trying new things and criticizing those who did try new things, such as body piercing, tattoos,, going to a nude beach, bungee jumping, ice fishing—you name it, anything that may not be what I would do but having little or no understanding of why others would want to do those things
- Not wanting to have kids—even when I was a child, wishing or desiring to be a parent was never even a consideration
- Blaming others for my actions or problems

Coping with Dysthymia

I wasn't sure how to cope with dysthymia. I'd made many changes in my life, such as believing in God and praying, that had helped in the past, but I wanted to do more for my own benefit.

When I started counseling, one of the first changes I made was to distance myself from other people's problems. Let them deal with their situations and I'd deal with mine.

I studied self-help, psychology, and spiritual books as well as CDs. For those of you who may not be spiritual or believe in the genius of Dr. Wayne Dyer as much as I do, I came across only two websites with information on coping with dysthymia. Here are the recommendations from the Mayo Clinic on coping with this mild form of depression:

1. Simplify your life. Cut back on obligations when possible, and set reasonable schedules for goals.

2. Write in a daily journal, expressing your pain, anger, fear, or other emotions as best as you can.
3. Read reputable self-help books and consider talking about them to your doctor or therapist.
4. Don't become isolated. Try to participate in normal activities and get together with family or friends regularly.
5. Join a support group for people with depression-related conditions so that you can connect to others facing similar challenges.
6. Stay focused on your goals. Recovery from dysthymia is an ongoing process. Stay motivated by keeping your recovery goals in mind. Remind yourself that you're responsible for managing your illness and working toward your goals.
7. Learn relaxation and stress management. Try stress-reduction techniques, such as meditation, yoga, or tai chi.
8. Structure your time. Plan your day and activities. Try to stay organized. You may find it helpful to make a list of daily tasks.

These additional coping strategies were laid out by www.depressionplace.com:

1. Learn to identify and cherish the small moments of joy in life. Look for the things that are wonderful in life, such as a good book, a flower, or a child's name.
2. Make sure to have plenty of comforting things around you, like fuzzy slippers, a warm blanket, or really good lasagna.
3. Get not only more sleep but more uninterrupted sleep. If you need help falling asleep, try music, a hot bath or shower, soothing aromatherapy candles, or lotions and comfortable pillows.
4. Turn to family and friends when you're feeling down, but avoid people who tend to be negative or critical.
5. Surround yourself with bright colors, even it means painting your walls or living space with bright colors.
6. Open your curtains, blinds, and shades … let the sunlight in.
7. Exercise daily, even if that may be just a walk around the block or the local mall. Fifteen minutes of exercise a day can improve your mood.

8. Don't forget to have a sense of humor. Watch humorous movies or sitcoms on TV, read a funny book, and seek out family and friends who will make you laugh.
9. Turn large tasks into smaller ones so you won't feel overwhelmed. Accomplish a little at a time instead of trying to do it all at one time.
10. Forgetfulness can be one of the more annoying symptoms of depression. If you are on several medications or if you have other health issues, it's a good idea to write it all down. Go to www.depressionplace.com/health_worksheet.html for a sample health worksheet.

Unaware of Depression?

How can someone live for more than four decades with dysthymia and not know something is wrong? The answer is quite simple: It is impossible for somebody to get behind another person's eyes or inside another person's brain. Therefore, if you grow up with depression, a mood disorder, ADHD (which is very common these days), or any other form of anxiety or mental disorder, how do you know you're not like everyone else?

Dysthymia was my "normal." I didn't know what it was like to be in someone else's mind, so I thought everyone was just like me. Even when others tell you something is wrong, you still believe you are normal. It wasn't until after my diagnosis and when I began taking medication that I truly felt normal, the chronic anger dissipated, and I felt like this must be how other people who don't have a depression disorder must live every day.

Which factors listed previously play a part in my dysthymic disorder? I suspect several, including genetics, upbringing, hormones, and neurotransmitters. The weird thing is, even when you see others reacting to situations completely different than you do, you have no control over what you feel and how you react. You know the right way to behave and think, but when it comes time to actually do it, you don't do the right thing; instead you do what you usually do. That in itself causes you more anger, anguish, and disgust. Your self-esteem sinks even lower than before. I knew I was different and didn't react normally, but I had no idea what to do about it or how to change.

Every year when my review at Disneyland was negative, I called home and complained to my mother. She, of course, supported me, saying they were way off base and didn't know what they were talking about. When the people closest to you offer no contradiction to your thoughts, supporting your delusions, those delusions become real in your mind.

If you are not the only one in your family suffering from the same or similar disorder they too will perceive events and respond to them in a similar fashion making these responses seem "normal" or ordinary, like everybody else. This in turn will make coming to terms with your illness and receiving a correct diagnosis almost impossible.

Have you ever heard the saying, "The definition of insanity is doing the same thing over and over again and expecting different results"? I look back now and know that I was indeed doing the same thing over and over again, expecting different results.

Chapter 7

Brain Transplant

With the Prozac prescription firmly in my hand, my husband and I silently walked side by side out of the waiting room of the psychiatrist's office, into the elevator, and out to the car. Breaking the silence, my husband finally asked, "So what did he say?"

I was ready to cry. Not out of depression but because I was relieved. Flooded by contradictory emotions of hope and slight disbelief that help was finally on its way, I told my husband all the details of the assessment as we made the long drive home.

We stopped by the pharmacy to drop off the prescription, and I spent all night perplexed about what life would be like for me when I wasn't depressed anymore. I wondered about the difference it would make in my mood, emotions, and feelings and how those changes might improve my life as a whole, including relationships with family and friends as well as my attitude toward life and all the ups and downs that come with it. Would my anger go away? Would I wake up happy instead of resentful over past wrongs? Would I like my life again? I couldn't wait to see and feel the effects of Prozac—and I wasn't disappointed.

Prozac is not the only antidepressant used to treat dysthymia. There are many, and your doctor or psychiatrist can prescribe the one that is best for you. Prozac just happens to be the one I tried first, and it bore amazing results. (According to the information included with my prescription, Prozac is also used to treat OCD, panic disorder, and bulimia nervosa in adults.)

Selective Serotonin Reuptake Inhibitor

Prozac is classified as a selective serotonin reuptake inhibitor (SSRI). Serotonin, according to www.webmd.com/depression/recognizing-depression-symptoms/serotonin acts as a neurotransmitter, a type of chemical that helps relay signals from one area of the brain to another. Although serotonin is manufactured in the brain, where it performs its primary functions, some 90 percent of our serotonin supply is found in the digestive tract and in blood platelets.

Serotonin either directly or indirectly affects most of the forty million brain cells people are estimated to have. These brain cells are related to mood, social behavior, appetite, sleep, memory, learning, and sexual desire and/or function. An imbalance or a lack of the necessary serotonin levels creates depression, anxiety, panic, and even excess anger.

An SSRI will prevent the body from reabsorbing the critical doses of serotonin in your brain that are needed to function normally and according to www.webmd.com, SSRIs are also being tested in relation to sudden infant death syndrome, dementia, and Alzheimer's disease.

Other chemicals in the brain, such as norepinephrine and dopamine, are related to sleep, voluntary movement, cognition, and memory. Medications containing these chemicals are currently used to treat Parkinson's disease, restless leg syndrome, ADHD, and fibromyalgia. (For more information go to www.about.com/chronicfatigue)

Tremors and Hallucinations

My first five days on Prozac weren't miserable, but I did experience a few bizarre and unexpected side effects. Have you known people who, as soon as they receive a new medication, they go directly to the side-effects portion of the drug monograph and start reading about all the bad things that might happen to them? I used to do that with every medication I took, but over time, I decided to just take whatever I needed to take and not worry about what the side effects might be.

However, with this medication, I did read the side effects. Some were very bizarre, such as abnormal dreams, hallucinations, and loss of memory, and some seemed rather expected or mild to me, such as dizziness, nausea, and diarrhea. I was certainly glad I read the side effects this time.

The second night, while I was sleeping, I had a tremor. My whole body shook for what seemed like several minutes and, while it was happening, I wondered if I was having some sort of seizure. Afterward I quickly fell back to sleep.

Remembering the tremor when I awoke the next morning, I kept it to myself, thinking, "No big deal. It was probably a one-time thing."

The next night, I did not have any seizures, but this time I experienced a bizarre dream. Because of my dream analysis earlier in the year, it had become a habit for me to relive my dreams as soon as I would wake up.

But with this dream, nothing came to me. I knew I had had a dream, or more than one, but I couldn't put a finger on what is was about. It seemed as though it was a second or even a millisecond of many dreams put together, like a collage you would see on TV where they flash the photos so fast you can't make out who was in them. My dream was like that. All through the next day, I tried to remember even a fraction of that dream, but I just couldn't do it.

The next two nights, I awoke in the middle of the night and in the morning with a pounding heartbeat. Not just a racing heart but a thundering "I feel like my heart is coming out of my chest" heartbeat. It was scary—downright terrifying, actually.

I immediately remembered the deep-breathing techniques I'd been practicing for the last year to relieve stress and anxiety. Within a minute or two of deep breathing, my racing, pounding heartbeat subsided. I could feel it slowing down, becoming weaker and less forceful. After a few minutes, my heartbeat returned to normal.

On top of the racing heartbeat, I also experienced a hallucination. Keep in mind, I'd never done recreational drugs. I'd never even smoked a cigarette or inhaled smoke from pot or other chemicals. Hallucinations were things other people felt and experienced because *they* were on drugs.

My husband had been snoring and I couldn't sleep, so I went to the living room to sleep on the sofa. About 2 a.m., I awoke and lifted my head to see my husband walking around, hunched over with a book in his hand. His feet were off the ground, and I could see right through him. He looked like a ghost from the Haunted Mansion at Disneyland: Blue, glowing, no bones, just a see-through hologram of a figure. If I had reached out to touch him, my hand would have gone straight through him.

I called out to him, but he never came. I called again and again, screaming, as I was scared to death. It was one of the most frightening, bizarre things I've ever experienced. I put my head on the pillow and fell asleep again, only to dream that my husband did come into the living room, sat beside me on the sofa, stroked my hair, and then proceeded to strangle and kill me.

When I awoke, I asked my husband if he'd heard me calling for him. He hadn't. After recounting my hallucination for him, he repeated that he never heard a thing and asked if I could have been dreaming the entire account. Then he asked, as only my husband could, "Do you have any more of that stuff?" as if he were interested in hallucinating as well.

To this day, I don't know for sure whether I hallucinated or dreamed of hallucinating. Either way, it was enough to scare me. I went to my desk and dug out the paperwork about Prozac that the pharmacy had given me. Under possible side effects were listed the mild ones, the ones I didn't have. And under that paragraph, in big, bold letters, it read "tell your doctor immediately if you have any of the following symptoms." That list included—you guessed it—tremors or shakes, hallucinations, rapid heartbeat, and abnormal dreams, just to name a few.

OK, that does it, I thought. Enough of this. I'm willing to tolerate a few side effects, but this is just getting too creepy and scary.

Early that morning, when I called the psychiatrist, he informed me that it was common for extremely anxious people to experience these weird side effects and that they would most likely disappear after my body and my brain acclimated to the drug. He gave me three choices:

1. Take another prescription for anxiety.
2. Try another anti-depressant altogether.
3. Take the Prozac once every other day for a week and then try it again every day in the hopes that smaller doses would give me time to adjust.

Within one week of taking the antidepressant only every other day, all my side effects disappeared. With the doctor's OK, my daily regimen of Prozac was restored. The bizarre dreams, hallucinations, and rapid heartbeat all went away and have never returned.

The recommended duration of time for taking antidepressants is eighteen months. After that, patients can slowly wean themselves off the medication to see if they still feel the same as when they were taking them. Some individuals feel the same months later, while others feel depressed again within a week.

Only time will tell what happens for me, and I'll be thrilled if I can live free of antidepressants. If not, I'm fine with that, too. If I have to stay on medication for the rest of my life, so be it, because I am not going back to being angry 24/7. Chronic anger, day in and day out, is more appalling, loathsome, and burdensome than you can realize if you've never experienced such a thing!

****

Being on a regular regimen of antidepressants is nothing short of miraculous to me. I'm amazed, grateful, and bewildered by the change and success this little pill has brought to my life. I feel like I've undergone a brain transplant, like someone else's mind has taken over my body. It's as if someone really did perform an exorcism on me in the middle of the night, extracting all the evil demons that had possessed me. I awoke one morning with a new life; the old, angry person was gone.

I no longer feel "mad for no reason" or plagued with unyielding, uncontrollable rage. I live in the moment, laugh more, worry less, and enjoy every day. The quality of my life has improved drastically, and everyone around me has not only noticed the difference but made comments to me about the difference.

It is hard to believe that just a few years back, I saw nothing to live for and wanted to die. How can one person's brain go from being in a deep dark, hole of hopelessness to one that is filled with positivity, joy, and anticipation of the future, no matter what it may bring? Just one pill to put everything back into its natural and proper balance, and someone can feel as if he or she has totally metamorphosed into the beautiful, free butterfly within.

As of today, I am the only person in my family to be officially diagnosed with dysthymia. I cannot say for sure if any other members of my immediate family have undiagnosed dysthymia, as I am not a mental health professional, and, to my knowledge, none of them has been evaluated by a psychiatrist.

However, several of my family members have little or no communication with others in the family due to arguments and being angry with one another long after the event has past. Since this disorder is genetic and hereditary, the odds are that I am not the only one with this condition. If others in the world are in denial, refusing to see that they need help for depression, or they refuse to take medications for fear of the side effects, I can only hope this book will help them.

I suspect that one of my second cousins on my mother's side had a form of depression. In 2009, seventy-two years old and still healthy, he believed he had nothing else to live for or accomplish and stopped eating. Family and friends tried to talk him out of it, but his mind was made up: He wanted to die.

As a kid, I remembered him being a strong and handsome man. He worked as a court reporter for most his life and drove a bright canary yellow Pantera sports car. But talking to this smart, successful man was another story altogether. Conversations with him were dominated by the negative side of politics, current events, sports, and other controversial topics. After an hour in this man's company, you felt hit by a siege of bad news coverage and hopelessness for the planet and everyone on it.

My cousin never married or had any children and gave all his money to charity except for a small amount he gave to each of his two sisters. After months of self-induced suffering, he died from starvation. We'll never know if he suffered from dysthmic disorder, but I will always wonder.

Chapter 8
No Coincidences

They say that when the student is ready, the teacher will appear. Over my two-year journey into therapy, I was ready to learn and be a student again. I was ready for anything and everything that would assist me in pulling myself up to a better place—a better mental place.

After all the struggles, counseling, and hopelessness, I ended up in a state of enlightenment. Enlightenment is the best place anyone can ever be, and you need not leave the house to find it.

Enlightenment, according to www.wikipedia.com, is "the full comprehension of a situation." In spiritual terms, the word alludes to a revelation or deep insight into the meaning and purpose of all things, communication with or understanding of the mind of God, profound understanding, or a fundamentally changed consciousness whereby everything is perceived as being unified.

My path to enlightenment was slow and gradual, with help and guidance from many individuals I do not know and probably will never meet. Piece by piece, I slowly put together my current thoughts, beliefs, and understanding as to why we are all here and the answer to that age-old question, "Why do bad things happen to good people?"

New-Age Spirituality

Hay House Publishing, its authors, and its radio programs are experts in new-age spirituality, self-improvement, and inspirational and transformational media. With the help of Dr. Wayne Dyer, Sylvia Browne, Louise Hay, and many others, my current beliefs about life, God, and even human suffering are extremely different from what they were when I was thirty. Their beliefs about God and the afterlife have given me a fresh, healthy, enjoyable, stronger, and more accepting attitude toward the reason and purpose of my life here on earth. Here are a few of the things I believe:

1. ***All human beings were with God before we came to this life.*** Every single one of us charted our life with God before coming to earth. We chose our parents; our height, weight, and hair and eye color; how smart we would be; how many children we'd have; where we'd go to school; and even how and when we would die. We agreed to life on earth to learn and grow for God After this process was finished, our memory of it was erased, and we were sent to Earth to follow our chart. Not knowing you are following a chart that you wrote is daunting to think about and puts all of us at a huge disadvantage while here on earth.
2. ***Luck, coincidences, and accidents do not exist.*** Everything is planned and charted down to the last detail. Everything that happens does so for a reason and a purpose, from sneezing to dropping an object to pain and suffering. You may not know the reason at the time something happens, but there is a reason.

   For example, in the 1990s, I did a lot of job seeking, did not own a computer, and needed someone to make my résumé look impressive and professional. I opened the phone book and hired the first "typing service" I could find. Over time, I realized how great this woman was with words, grammar, spelling, and editing and went back to her several times. I truly believed I met this woman for that very reason.

   However, when *Born Mad* was only a few paragraphs long, I knew I would need an editor. The first person who came to mind was Lynette. Today, I know the real reason I met Lynette was so I'd have an editor for *Born Mad,* not to create a résumé twenty years ago.
3. ***The world and the universe work according to God's plan, not the way you or I think it should be.*** God hears all your prayers; however, he can and does say no on more than one occasion. If what you ask for does not come your way, don't fret, because what does come your way is exactly what was

supposed to; it was in your chart. You are to learn something from it. The old saying, "When one door closes, another opens" is true. You just have to believe it is true. When you come to realize that God's plan and your plan are exactly the same, you'll worry less. You will have less anxiety, and many of your fears will subside. Believe in the plan for your peace of mind. The universal plan works every minute of every day, and if you open your mind and your eyes, you'll see it working throughout your life.

4. ***See your mistakes as an opportunity for growth.*** Pick yourself up, try again, and do it better next time. Everyone makes mistakes, it's how we learn and grow.
5. ***Blame, shame, guilt, jealousy, and resentment are harmful, useless emotions that serve no purpose.*** Rid your mind, spirit, and ego of these things. These emotions will only hurt you and those you love. They offer no benefit of any kind to any one.
6. ***No one religion is correct or incorrect.*** They all have merit, value, and truth. Believe whatever you want to believe, as long as you are not hurting anyone else in the process and your beliefs help you along the way to make it through this "boot camp" called life.
7. ***There are no justified resentments.*** The only person you hurt by being bitter and resentful is yourself. Forgive everyone for everything. That doesn't mean you have to be their friend or have a relationship with them no matter what, but do forgive and move on.
8. ***Your "little voice" or "intuition" is God talking to you.*** You've heard the saying that your first choice is usually right. It is, so go with it. That voice is God telling you what to do, giving you answers, advice, and guidance about your problems, dilemmas, and daily decisions.
9. ***We all have past lives.*** We've all been male, female, black, white, skinny, obese, gay, and straight. You'll be all these things at one time before you are on your last life. Rid yourself of prejudice, as the very same hate may come your way in another life.
10. ***All beings are connected.*** All humans are entwined with one another, and the actions of one will affect the actions

of another. The decisions you make today will affect future generations to come, even people living in others countries whom you've never met or don't know about.

11. ***Your ego really is your worst enemy.*** We all do bad, hurtful things because we let our ego get in the way. We don't want to be wrong or look weak or stupid, and we don't want others to view us as incompetent or not good enough. Our ego drives us to these thoughts, for at certain times, we are all wrong, incompetent, and not as good as others in some areas. It's called being human.
12. ***The human body is a garage that stores and contains your spirit while you are here on earth.*** We all grow old and wrinkled and put on weight. We will eventually be unable to do many of the things we used to when we were younger. But that's OK. What matters is how young, vibrant, and alive you feel inside. All of us will leave our body behind when we die because it isn't the important part of who you are. What's inside, how you treat others, and your character and integrity are what matters. That doesn't mean you shouldn't treat your body with love and care for it properly. It is your vehicle and in order for it to work properly, you must maintain it the best you can. Exercise, eating a healthful diet, and avoiding drugs and alcohol will make your outer shell work properly and last longer.
13. ***God loves everyone equally.*** Have you ever heard someone inquire about why bad things happen to good people or why good things happen to bad people? First, good and bad are judgments, and God does not make judgments. (He wouldn't be perfect if He did, right?) Labeling something as "good" or "bad" is a human attribute, not an attribute of God. Bad things happen to people—all people. And good things happen to people—all people. Whether a good or bad event happens has nothing to do with whether someone is "good" or "bad."

    Second, whatever events happen in your life, good or bad, you agreed to them. You picked them so you could advance and expand mentally and emotionally. If everybody and everything were perfect and mistakes did not exist, we'd all be stuck in the same place—in limbo, if you will.

14. ***When "bad" things happen, something good always follows.*** This continues the previous thought. When something bad happens, you may not see it right away, but something good will come of it. For instance, if you are familiar with the show *America's Most Wanted*, then you know the host, John Walsh. In 1981, Walsh's son, Adam, was kidnapped from a Sears department store in Hollywood FL. Sixteen days later, Adam was found brutally murdered and his body dumped one hundred twenty miles from the family's home.

    Following the death of their son, Walsh and his wife founded the Adam Walsh Child Resource Center, a nonprofit organization dedicated to legislative reform regarding missing and exploited children. In 1988, Walsh was selected to host *America's Most Wanted,* which today is the longest-running television show in Fox network history. More than 1,000 fugitives have been captured after their profile was made public on this series. (http://en.wikipedia.org/wiki/John_Walsh)

    Did Walsh and his family know that something positive would come from Adam's death? I doubt it. They probably felt it was the worst event in their lives, and they no doubt paid a huge price for what happened. But with that huge price came a foundation that was desperately needed, major changes in laws and legislation regarding abducted children, and a television show that has successfully put thousands of felons behind bars. Something "good" did come out of something "bad."

    Have faith and confidence and believe that whatever it is you're going through, you'll come out better for it in the end.

15. ***We are all doing the best we can with the knowledge we have at the time.*** Forgiveness is essential for this reason. No one likes to make mistakes, use poor judgment, or "screw things up." But all of us do according to what information is available to us and what we know how to do.

New Positive Beliefs

Remember those negative, sarcastic, self-defeating thoughts mentioned in Chapter 2? If you use any of them, try replacing them with more meaningful, positive, and beneficial thoughts, such as the following:

"The early bird gets the worm."

"It's not whether you win or lose, but how you play the game that counts."

"If you can't say something nice, don't say anything at all."

"If at first you don't succeed, try, try again."

"From all things bad comes something good."

"When one door closes, another one opens."

"Life is 10 percent what happens to you and 90 percent how you deal with it."

I can't change the family patterns I grew up with, but I can and have changed how I react to them today. The constant "zingers" have faded away, as I no longer feel better about myself by insulting or making fun of others. I force myself to keep an open mind about others and why people might engage in behaviors I may not wish to or agree with, and I try not to pass judgment on them for doing so. Living in the moment with an open mind, devoid of criticism and expectations of others, has led me to a more happy, productive, and enjoyable life.

Doing The Work by Byron Katie

Every day, we have thoughts that may or may not be true. And even though our thoughts may not be true, we still tend to believe them. This, in and of itself, can be destructive and lead to judgmental, self-defeating attitudes and actions.

One of best self-help authors and speakers I've found is a woman named Byron Katie. After years of dealing with depression and thoughts of suicide, she created The Work (www.thework.com), and it has been compared to the works of Buddhist teachings and twelve-step programs. It is a way to help individuals find peace and happiness within themselves and in the world in which they live.

Today, in my head, I review the four questions from The Work with almost every thought that comes to my mind. After answering the four questions, I usually know what to do. The four questions are:

1. Is it true?
2. Can you absolutely know it is true?
3. How do you react, what happens when you believe that thought?
4. Who would you be without that thought?

Then, she says to turn around the concept you're questioning, finding at least three genuine, specific examples of how the turnaround is true in your life..

This small but powerful tool botched my anniversary vacation in August 2010. My husband and I were about a mile down the road from our house when he said, "Don't be surprised if we get stopped by a cop for not having a license plate on the trailer." We were pulling our Jet Ski so we could use it on Lake Ozarka, and the license plate was nailed onto the left wheel well. It was visible, but from a distance ,the trailer looked like it had no license plate.

Trying to be less neurotic, I had just been doing The Work exercises. When my husband made the comment about getting pulled over, I asked him why he would say that. He could have started our trip with a positive thought like "The trip will be pleasant and nothing will go wrong," or he could have started with a negative thought, like "We are going to get pulled over."

I answered "The Work" questions in my head. Was it true? Did I know for sure we would be pulled over by a cop? Answer to both: No.

Now, how did I feel about both those thoughts? I felt neurotic and paranoid, thinking we would be pulled over by a cop. That thought ruined my trip before it even started. However, if I believed we wouldn't be pulled over, or the thought never even entered my mind, I would have a peaceful, happy trip and would feel less neurotic and more stable, like I was living in the moment. I was happier just driving down the street and not thinking of "possibilities."

But my husband wasn't thrilled about my newfound knowledge like I was, and an argument ensued. He was trying to make conversation, whereas I just wanted a peaceful, fun trip, free of "what-ifs." But my husband took my part of the conversation as criticism when I thought I was just trying to help to improve our daily attitude about life, and it ruined our trip to Lake Ozarka.

I'm thrilled to have found Byron Katie, even if it means annoying my husband on occasion. In fact, when I'm able to catch myself thinking negatively, I automatically turn them around. For example, I could say to myself, "I'll never get my book published; no one will want to read it." Instead, I ask myself, "Do I know absolutely 100 percent, without a doubt that no one will want to read this book?" Answer: No, I can't know that without a doubt.

Now, I turn the thought around. I tell myself *Born Mad* is of great value, and many people would love to read about my struggle and how I overcame depression, fear, and anger. Who am I with the positive thought? I am a new author, a writer overjoyed at the thought of seeing my book in print and sold in retail stores and as an e-book on the Internet. With that thought, I am free and succeeding in a new challenge I never thought I would even attempt. My spirit feels better with the positive thought than with the negative one. So today, I choose to run with the thought that makes me feel better about myself and others.

If you have a choice between a self-defeating thought and a self-improving thought, choose the latter. Make the better choice, the one that makes you feel good about yourself. Don't choose the one that makes you feel worthless or not good enough. I did that for too long and now choose to live the rest of my years with thoughts that make me feel happy, with a purpose and meaning, uplifting spirits and encouraging others.

Chapter 9
It's All Small Stuff

A few days before Christmas 2010, I visited the psychiatrist for the third time. He no longer needed to take notes on the events in my life, and we both could sit down and chat for a few minutes about my current state of mind without quizzes or rehashing past events.

He asked me how I felt, if I found activities that gave me pleasure, and if I was satisfied with my marriage. Then he asked, "Now that the medication has had time to take effect, do you feel back to your normal self? Do you feel like you did before?" I answered, "No, and I hope I never do."

The psychiatrist looked puzzled, maybe even a little disappointed. But I followed it up with an explanation: "I've never felt this way ever in my entire life. I am certain I was born with dysthymia because my life now is something I have never experienced before. It's as if I have been given a second life, a second chance to get things right, a second brain and soul to guide me because the first one wasn't working correctly."

Reflecting on the Changes

You see, on Prozac, I finally feel like other people who don't suffer with chronic, habitual anger and depression issues. Every day is the same: good. Great, actually. Little things no longer bother me or get me down. And better yet, I am able to recognize just about everything as a "little thing," whereas before all things were huge and of dire importance. All those affirmations and sayings I'd worked on that helped only when I was in a good mood, but didn't work at all when I was down, are now taking a solid hold over my thoughts and emotions. Every day is a good day.

My life is vastly different today, even though relatively little has changed. I'm married to the same man, have the same career as a wildlife educator, and have the same family and friends. I live in the same town and the same house as before, yet I experience joy every day, living anger free with a new, positive outlook on life. With the help of antidepressants and self-help affirmations, the raging, emotionally unbalanced, and detrimental thoughts I had toward myself and others are gone. My body now has adequate amounts of serotonin, and those mean "tapes" that played in my head over and over again have been replaced by better thoughts.

The dysthymia diagnosis opened windows for me, and I now understand why I spent so many years feeling like life was difficult and I was swimming upstream. Life was always an uphill battle because the coping mechanisms I needed to deal with adversity were not there.

Life today is not a struggle. It is easier and more enjoyable, and I no longer feel like I constantly make mistakes.

I grew up believing that life is 90 percent of what happens to you and 10 percent how you deal with it. When bad things happen, I thought you should complain so everyone would feel sorry for you and solve all your problems.

Today, I know that life is only 10 percent what happens to you and 90 percent how you deal with it. Now, being more balanced, calm, and mentally and emotionally stable, I can utilize the same logic, reasoning, and rational thoughts that were used for coping with adversity by those folks in my past who I believed were "swimming with the current."

Today, the only anger I deal with relates to fleeting, occasional occurrences, the kind "normal, nonangry" people deal with. The moments where you say, "Oh darn, I forgot my wallet" or when the cook at a restaurant gets your order wrong. I now recognize those things as small and insignificant and no longer sweat it when my dinner doesn't come out exactly right. Find a way to learn to not sweat the small stuff. (See the Related Resources section for Richard Carlson's *Don't Sweat the Small Stuff Workbook*) Thankfully, I now look at just about everything as "small stuff."

I've also decided to seek out a few relatives and friends with whom I haven't spoken in years. As I was writing *Born Mad* and recalled their contributions to my life as a young child, I realized I missed their presence in my life. So I contacted my aunt and uncle on my father's side of the family and arranged for a visit. Despite the fact they lived in Northern California, just a few hours' drive away when I resided in Orange County,

California, I never really made an effort to visit them. But I wanted to know them better and felt I had been shortchanged by not socializing with them more often after my parents divorced. Now, I make an effort to fly to California and stay with them for a few days out of the year, and it is a decision I am delighted to have made.

After writing the "Firebucket" story, I remember how much fun my sister and I had as kids, playing with our godbrothers and godsisters. We'd spend weekends and holidays at each other's houses, braiding each other's hair, staying up late telling spooky stories, and riding bikes and skating around the block until we were too tired to do it anymore. So I looked up one of my godsisters, and we e-mail and talk on the phone regularly. She, too, has many happy memories of when we were kids, including Mr. and Mrs. Crabtree, who lived behind my house. Their name really wasn't Crabtree, but they were an elderly couple and when we would hit our baseball over the fence into their backyard and accidentally brake a flower pot, one of them would come out and scold us for doing so. They were mean to all the kids, and we dreaded walking around the block to knock on their door to retrieve out baseball. We'd take turns getting our ball back and then repeat the entire conversation when we got home. After a while, we nicknamed them "Mr. and Mrs. Crabtree."

After I was diagnosed with dysthymia and began taking a daily dose of Prozac, I decided not to pursue a divorce, a career change, or living in another country. My irritability and intolerance for everything that was bothering me subsided, and I realized they didn't really matter anyway. I realized how much I loved and adored my life and my wonderful, loving husband. We get along better now (because I am not nagging and cranky anymore), love each other for who we are, and do not try to change one other. We laugh more and spend more time just relaxing on the porch swing, playing cards or watching TV.

I love psychology, soaking up anything and everything regarding human behavior and improving thought patterns and relationships with friends and family.

I no longer need to win an argument or a game or be "the best" at something; I just want to have fun and enjoy life. Attempting to be "better" than someone else is futile because if you compete with one person, then you have to compete with everyone, and that's a losing proposition from the start. Winning, no matter what is also not very kind, as no one on earth is better than anyone else for any reason.

I no longer wish to be a perfectionist, hypersensitive, strongly opinionated, or a workaholic. All those things create imbalance and a sense of entitlement and self-righteousness. Proving I'm right is unimportant, and I frequently practice saying "I don't know" instead to maintain peace. We all know very little, and no one can afford to be arrogant, thinking he or she knows everything.

I take more time off from work now. Since I have my own business and make my own schedule, I can take off a whole week or month or just an evening to go out to dinner and catch a movie. The lake is nearby; I'd rather spend time on the boat or riding a Jet Ski than working a sixteen-hour day. Living a happy, fun life sounds more appealing to me than making the almighty dollar. I'd rather live a more simple life and spend more time with my family and friends than have a Rolex or a large-screen HDTV.

Today, I'm happy knowing I have no control over others, the planet, or what happens in the future. I take life one day at a time and do not get upset over things I hear on the news, such as the Enron scandal or famous athletes cheating on their spouses. Once, I heard someone say, "There are three kinds of business: yours, other people's, and God's." You are not entitled to any of these except your own. Your business is *your* business. Natural disasters are God's business, and the rest is other people's business. You can't do anything about any of it except what you have control over. Individuals can control only their thoughts and emotions, how they perceive things, and how they react to them. You will never have control over others' actions, thoughts, or feelings.

Thanks to the help of Dr. Wayne Dyer, Sylvia Browne, and www.hayhouse.com, I am no longer afraid to die. Death is not the end but a beginning of a new, better, and different life. We will all be surrounded by love, forgiveness, and compassion; hate, violence, and mental disorders, such as dysthymia, depression, OCD, and schizophrenia, will not exist in the next life. Human egos will not ruin or taint the environment because we all coexist peacefully without the misconception that we are or have to be better than everyone else.

Before 2009, I couldn't see God at all. Now, not only do I believe in God, but I see God in everything. I see God in trees, animals, music, and everything else on this planet, as well as in people of all sexes, creeds, religions, races, colors, and sexual orientation. God is responsible for what most people call "coincidences" or "luck." All of us—whether young, old, overweight, or bulimic—are here to serve a purpose; our differences and imperfections were given to us so we could learn to grow and love.

Today, I am still not a churchgoer. After about twenty minutes of listening to a sermon and sitting in one spot, I am bored to tears, stiff all over, and antsy to leave. I still believe in God, but I do my praying at home and have eliminated the idea that church is somewhere I must go to be happy or am obligated to attend services as a means to get into heaven. Everybody on the planet can have a connection with God, no matter where they are or who they're with. Church is not crucial or essential to being spiritual.

Born Mad would not be complete without mentioning my husband's part in all of this. Most marriage vows say "for better or for worse, in sickness and in health, for richer or poorer." My husband is the prime example of this. I put him through hell, nagged and complained to him about things I thought he did wrong, and only rarely thanked him for his help and assistance. He was (and still is) helpful around the house, supportive of everything I want to try or learn or create, and he never complained when I fell apart and wanted to move out. He held me when I cried, woke up at all hours of the night to comfort me, and protected me when I couldn't do it myself. Without him, my new life, *Born Mad*, and my newfound happiness would not have been possible.

Life could not have been easy for him, either. When you go through mental grief and turmoil, the pain, fear, and unhappiness is so profound that it is almost impossible to think about or comprehend the pain, anxiety, and agony you've caused the people around you. I have no doubt that dealing with me, sticking by me, and not wanting to be furious at me was not an easy task.

I'm extremely fortunate (I don't believe in luck, so I won't say I'm lucky) to have a spouse who could understand I was in more pain than he was. He put aside his feelings and dealt with whatever he had to endure, knowing I was suffering much more than he was. Forgiveness and compassion were his strengths, as he never got angry with me or badmouthed me to anyone for feeling like I did. For those of you going through the same turmoil I did, I hope you have someone like my husband by your side to help and guide you through it. It will become one more item to add to your gratitude journal.

New Habits and Thoughts

Today, I practice habits and thoughts that are totally different from my previous ones. Here's a list of my new, everyday, top 10 thoughts and habits that have improved my quality of life:

1. ***Every day, I say my prayers in the morning and before going to sleep.*** I thank God for all he has given me and rarely ask for anything in return. Basically, I do my gratitude journal mentally and to God. I may ask for him to watch over someone who is ill as well as his or her family, and I ask for his protection, blessing, guidance, and forgiveness for everyone on the planet. But I never ask for a nicer car, more money, or a bigger house. I have everything I need. They say that the key to life is not having what you want but wanting what you have.
2. ***Every day, I remind myself that everyone on this earth is equal, special, and worthy.*** No one person is better than another or entitled to something others aren't entitled to, for we are all entitled to absolutely nothing. Everything we have or want has to be earned.
3. ***I do something spiritual every day.*** Whether it is listening to www.hayhouseradio.com or any of my numerous CDs to reading a self-help book or my Wayne Dyer calendar, I try to partake in something that makes me feel good about life, others, and myself.
4. ***I've cut my time in front of the TV in half.*** I omit the crime dramas and real-life murder stories on shows such as *City Confidential* and *Dateline.* I watch shows that make me feel good and are pleasant, such as the reality dance shows. I take time to read from a book every day instead of sitting in front of the TV.
5. ***I exercise, exercise, exercise.*** I try to walk three miles and/or ride a stationary bike for thirty to forty-five minutes several times a week. I have a treadmill and a stationary bike in the living room and I have a park pass, so when the weather is nice, I can get back to nature while exercising outdoors.
6. ***I remind myself to tame my ego.*** I am not always right; I do not know everything. In fact, I know very little about any subject you could think of discussing and what I believe about that subject may not be right. My opinions are irrelevant unless someone asks me, and even then I try to not have an opinion. I would rather look at both sides of the coin and be open minded about something than to believe my opinion is

the only correct way of thinking or doing something. Life is not about me or about you, and if you live in "me" mode all the time, you lose your gratitude, appreciation, and compassion. Been there, done that, don't want it ever again.

7. ***I try to meditate every day.*** I'm not as diligent as I used to be, but after my prayers at night, I lie in bed and try to quiet my mind. Focusing for a long time on one thing is a bit difficult for me, so I usually cannot mediate for twenty or thirty minutes, as I start thinking of other things and have to pull myself back to a quiet, still mind. I attempt to think of nothing, quieting my mind and being still for even a few minutes. And I don't watch the news before going to bed. Dr. Dyer calls this "the last five minutes of your day." The goal is to avoid ruminating on all the things that happened during the day, all the chores you need to do tomorrow, or all the problems in our society which are so often shown on the nightly news. The goal is to have the last five minutes of your day be peaceful, positive, and beneficial to your mental, emotional, and physical health. So I try to think of as little as possible.
8. ***I forgive everyone for everything, as there are no justified resentments.*** Resentment causes anger, anger causes rage, rage causes violence, and violence causes more harm than can be discussed here. Forgive everyone—this doesn't mean you have to forget—and live in the present moment, for it is the only moment you have. Forgiveness is the key to life. When you do not forgive yourself or others, the only damage you do is to yourself, not to the person you refuse to forgive.
9. ***I dumped the daily sugar habit.*** People who suffer from anxiety benefit from a healthful diet of protein, fiber,fruits, and vegetables. My sugar consumption has diminished greatly, as has my caffeine intake. I love chocolate and will probably never cut that out entirely. Once a week, I like to treat myself, but I don't eat dessert after every meal like I used to.
10. ***Every day, I make an effort to not call others names, degrade them, or think I am better just because they may do or say something I don't understand.*** If, at family dinners, the conversation turns to complaining and criticism, I don't participate. Yet we all, at one time or another, call another

person a name. I used to do it all the time. Someone does something or says something we don't understand, and we immediately call them stupid, an idiot, a freak, a jackass, or something similar. Be aware that these words, criticisms, and complaints about others are used to make individuals feel superior to others and therefore better about themselves.

11. ***I am no longer afraid to say no.*** In fact, I've learned I can say no without feeling the need to give an explanation. The only real way to respect yourself is to be able to say no when you're asked to do something that is not in your best interest. If you give everyone what they want just because they asked for it, then you'll end up ignoring what you desire and want to do. You'll live your life for others, not for yourself. You'll become a sellout, and being a sellout will leave you bitter and resentful.

Will I be thrilled to have diabetes in the future? No, of course not. However, I hope that now I can handle whatever health issues come my way with dignity and grace and realize that something good will come from it. No matter what ails you, you still have to live the rest of your life as joyfully and enthusiastically as possible. The only thing one is guaranteed is the here and now. No tomorrows or next year, just today, right now. Perhaps you'll agree that the "miserable route" isn't any way to live your life. Dr. Dyer says a person should be willing to let anything happen, good or bad. I want this to be my new motto for life.

If I hadn't lived more than half my life making huge mistakes (not to mention making a complete ass of myself) and hadn't been angry since birth, I would never have been depressed or suicidal. If I hadn't been depressed, suicidal, and angry, I wouldn't have sought help. Without help, I never would have found out I had been living with dysthymia for more than forty years. Without my diagnosis, I would not have felt compelled to write this book. Without writing this book, I would never have been able to help others or shed light on a basically unknown disease that many others have but may be unaware of. If *Born Mad* helps one person, telling my story of pain and anger will be worth it. If *Born Mad* helps many people, I'll be thrilled and eternally grateful.

If one event in my life had been different, most likely none of this would have come to pass. It is true: Your life is a journey, and all you can do is go where it takes you. You might have had different plans for yourself—I know I did—but what is happening to you now is supposed to happen. And it is happening for a reason and a purpose. Do you know at the time a certain event is happening why it is happening and what the reason or purpose is? Maybe you do, maybe you don't. Even if it is a mystery to you, go where it takes you.

When people think with their emotions instead of their intellect, frustration and anxiety take over. When frustration and anxiety take over, people almost always make a decision that compounds their current situation and makes things worse than before, like life is spinning out of control and nothing swings in your favor or works out the way you wish or expect.

If people who are unable to make decisions repeatedly turn to friends and/or family for advice or to help solve their problems, they become a burden to everyone around them. As someone who was confused and troubled by the smallest of situations, I was a burden to my family and friends. With the help of Prozac, enlightenment, a belief in God, and an "I can do it!" attitude, I hope I am no longer that burden. When a decision needs to be made, I ignore how I feel and focus instead on logic to determine what choice would be more beneficial to me and my family and how to achieve the best possible outcome.

The human body and psyche are actually very amazing if you think about it. People often say, without really thinking, "If that happens, I'll just die." The truth is, we suffer a great deal throughout our lives, enduring an incredible amount of physical and emotional stress and anguish, and yet many of us live to see another day and even tell our story to others. We all withstand a lot more than what we think we can endure. They say that whatever doesn't kill you only makes you stronger. But I think it would more appropriate to say, if you don't have an undiagnosed mental disorder, whatever doesn't kill you only makes you stronger. According to www.save.org, more than one million people worldwide commit suicide every year. Suicide is the eleventh cause of death in the U.S. and the strongest factor for suicide is depression. An average of one person dies by suicide every 16.2 minutes. But 80 percent of people who seek treatment for depression are treated successfully and suicide can be prevented through education and public awareness. Please do not be one of these sad statistics. Seek help and keep seeking until you find peace and happiness. Be part of the 80 percent who conquer their depression.

When this book was just a mere thought, an idea to play with, I said to myself, "I am an author, I am an author, I am an author." I pictured what the cover would look like, looked for an editor, and pictured my books being sold in bookstores and on the internet. I did these things because Dr. Wayne Dyer would tell me to. I pictured it and acted accordingly. When you believe it, you will see it. And I believe.

Conclusion
Peace and Happiness

In the foreword, my husband mentioned my courage and determination. As the events of my life were unfolding, I didn't feel courageous at all. I felt like a wimp, a wuss, someone who was unable to handle minor things that other people seem to handle with ease. My determination just felt like survival to me. I hated being angry, mean, and hateful. I needed to find a solution if I was going to live a life that was better than what I had.

Some professionals might believe that no one can be born mad, but I disagree. Since dysthymia is genetic and I've had many of the symptoms of dysthymia since birth or early childhood, I believe it is possible to be "born mad."

Do I think all angry people have dysthymia and need medication? No, of course not. It just happened to be what worked for me after trying numerous therapies that failed one right after another. But if you have tried anger management classes with no improvement and don't feel better or less angry, then try something else. Try anything and everything until you find something that works.

There are people in this world who have been through trials and tribulations much tougher than mine. I consider myself extremely fortunate, as I never resorted to drugs, alcohol, or violence. But my rage was real and festered for years without my knowing it. Our society—our planet—needs more information about this odd and vague disorder and about anger, what causes it, and how to get rid of it. More information by people who have it, have lived through it, and recovered through whatever means possible can only benefit generations to come.

Today, we observe a lot of rage in people around the world. Just turn on the news and you'll hear it. Celebrities being tape recorded while having fits of rage and swearing at others or everyday folks beating up, shooting, and attacking others for a wrong they think occurred. I don't have all the answers regarding why people do these things, and I never will.

All I can do is write my story, put it out there, and see if someone else felt and lived through the same thing. My inability to forgive others, let go of past events, and reverse my negative feelings and resentment were due to excessive anger caused by a mental illness. All these things became harmful and dangerous to me and others around me. Now, with the help of an SSRI that allows my body to maintain normal levels of serotonin, I feel like a completely different person. With ease, I forgive and let bygones be bygones. When unfortunate events happen, I look for the lesson I need to learn in order to grow with this new experience and to move on to the next one, loving those in my life no matter what they do. And most of all, I've learned to forgive myself. You cannot forgive others if you cannot forgive yourself.

In the middle of writing *Born Mad*, three events occurred. First, I was finally able to find a book about dysthmia written by someone who actually has the disease, suffered through the day-to-day aspects of it, and actually knows what it feels like. Vivian Eisenecher suffered for years with social phobia, alcoholism, and depression. Her book, *Recovering Me, Discovering Joy,* is listed in the Books and CDs subsection of Related Resources at the back of this book.

Second, the last session with my therapist took place on January 12, 2011. We both agreed that with the medication, I've finally defeated the chronic anger that was plaguing my thoughts, emotions, and life in general. Ending therapy was a little bittersweet for me, as my therapist was compassionate, smart, and fun to be around and talk to. She had many qualities that would make her a great friend. She was my first choice to write the foreword to *Born Mad;* however, it would have been considered a breach of her professional ethics, so she was forced to deny my request. But knowing that I had defeated my anger issues, gained self-confidence, and no longer felt like I wanted to be someone else far outweighs the negative aspects of leaving therapy. It is a great comfort to be out on my own again, so to speak, and not feel as if I need counseling to get through everyday life.

Third, while reading Eisenecher's book, I noticed she cited www.psychcentral.com as a reference. Out of curiosity, I logged on and found more than thirty self-questionnaires about behavior, ranging from mania, eating disorders, OCD, sexual addiction, and adult-onset attention-deficit disorder. My husband and I both took several of the quizzes. I don't tend to stay put for very long and lose interest in activities, such as reading a book, working on an art project, or watching TV, before I ever complete them. My self-evaluations showed it was "not probable" that I was a narcissist or had any anxiety issues or autism but showed a "good probability" for OCD and ADHD.

These quizzes, of course, are not meant to take the place of an evaluation by a mental healthcare professional. They might, however, give you a tool or resource to lead you in the right direction if you should seek professional help.

The authors at Hay House and a regular regimen of antidepressants saved my life, my marriage, my job, and my sanity. When you hear about a person having a mental disorder, you tend to associate it with a bad stigma, believing that person is crazy and should be in an institution. But today, that is just not the case. If you are diagnosed with a mood or depression disorder, it is not your fault. Don't let society or social norms make you feel embarrassed or ashamed. Instead, talk about what is bothering you and how you are feeling because there are others out there feeling and thinking the same things. They can offer beneficial support and advice that people who don't suffer from the same disorder cannot offer or understand. Since 2010, I have searched for such a support group for dysthymic disorder but have been unable to find one—hence, my goal of creating one myself.

If you suffer from depression, anxiety, excess anger, or frustration, there is hope for you, too. Don't give up. Keep seeking and searching for options. When the agony of your mere existence becomes overwhelming, you will be willing to try anything. If you are willing to try whatever it takes to rid yourself of your anger, anxiety, and depression, you will find a solution. And above all, it is what you are meant to go through. You may not find the purpose until months or years later, but there is a hidden meaning behind all of it. I wish peace and happiness to all.

Related Resources

Associations

American Psychiatric Association, 1000 Wilson Blvd, Suite 1825, Arlington, VA 22209-3901; Phone: 703-907-7300

National Anger Management Association, 2753 Broadway, Suite 395, New York, NY 10025; Phone: 646-485-5116; Fax: 646-390-1571 (The association has a specialist directory for the United States, Japan, Canada, the United Kingdom, Italy, and Puerto Rico.)

Books and CDs

Browne, Sylvia. 2007. *Spiritual Connections: How to Find Spirituality Throughout All the Relationships in Your Life.* Carlsbad, CA: Hay House, Inc.

Carlson, Richard. 1998. *Don't Sweat the Small Stuff Workbook.* New York, NY: Hyperion.

Carnegie, Dale. 1988. *How to Win Friends & Influence People.* New York, NY: Simon & Schuster, Inc

Dyer, Wayne. 1995. *101 Ways to Transform Your Life.* Carlsbad, CA: Hay House, Inc.

Dyer, Wayne. 1993. *Everyday Wisdom.* Carlsbad, CA: Hay House, Inc.

Dyer, Wayne. 2011. *Excuses Be Gone! How to Change Lifelong, Self-Defeating Thinking Habits.* Carlsbad, CA: Hay House, Inc.

Dyer, Wayne. 1987. *How to Be a No-Limit Person.* Niles, IL: Nightingale-Conant, Inc.

Eisenecher, Vivian. 2008. *Recovering Me, Discovering Joy.* San Diego, CA: KTW Publishing

Gentry, W. Doyle. 2006. *Anger Management for Dummies.* Hoboken, NJ: Wiley Publishing, Inc.

McGraw, Phil. 2008. *Real Life.* New York, NY: Simon & Schuster, Inc

Peale, Norman Vincent. 1992. *The Power of Positive Thinking.* New York, NY: Simon & Schuster, Inc.

Hotlines

Depression Hotline: 630-482-9696

Suicide Hotline: 800-SUICIDE (800-784-2433)

Teen Suicide Hotline: 800-784-2433

Websites

www.anger-management-resources.org for the Anger Management Resource Directory

www.beliefnet.com to test your religious beliefs and compare to more than 25 different religions

www.depression-guide.com for information on depression

www.depressionstatistics.org for information on depression

www.health.harvard.edu/newsweek/dysthymia.html for information about dysthmia

www.mayoclinic.com/health/dysthymia.com for support and tips on coping with dysthymia www.mentalhealth.com for a free encyclopedia of mental health information

www.namass.org for the National Anger Management Association, a place to get help

www.psychcentral.com for PsychCentral, a mental health and psychology network with quizzes, blogs, and other resources

www.similarminds.com to take a personality test

www.thework.com for Byron Katie's "The Work"

www.vaxa.com for a list of organizations that help with depression and suicide

www.webmd.com for information about dysthymia and depression

www.webmd.com/depression.com for recognizing signs of depression

www.yellowribbon.org for the Yellow Ribbon Suicide Prevention Program

Other Anger-Causing Disorders

According to www.bettermedicine.com, www.wrongdiagnosis.com and www.wikipedia.com, here are a few other physical and mental disorders that may cause excess anger.

Psychriatric causes

Borderline Personality Disorder

Childhood Depression

Manic Depression or Bipolar

Cyclothymia

Oppositional Defiant Disorder

Severe Depression

Premenstrual Dysphoric Disorder

Intermittent Explosive Disorder (characterized by extreme anger)

Organic Personality Syndrome

Schizophrenia

Post-Traumatic Stress Disorder

Attention Deficit Disorder

Autism

Antisocial Personality Disorder

Dementia (including Alzheimer's and Huntington's disease)

Conduct Disorder (behavior disorder in childhood)

Physical Causes and Other Diseases or Conditions

Epilepsy

Lead poisoning

Brain tumors

Head injury

Smoking cessation

Alcohol or Drug Addiction

Hypoglycemia (low blood sugar)

Meningitis

Tuberous sclerosis (childhood episodes of screaming)

About the Author

An avid animal lover since childhood, Robyn Wheeler created a wildlife education company in 1996 called The Creature Teacher, LLC. Based in East Texas, Robyn travels throughout the state, presenting various animal-related shows to children and adults of all ages at local schools, libraries, and birthday parties. She graduated from California State Polytechnic University, Pomona in 1988, worked at Disneyland as an animal caretaker for eleven years, and was an Orange County Animal Control Officer for two years. Before starting her own business, she taught an animal-care class to high school students for the Regional Occupations Center of Garden Grove. Robyn now lives on nine acres with her husband, Ron, and calico cat, Zoey.